YOUNG READERS' EDITION

AMERICAN MOONSHOT

John F. Kennedy and the Great Space Race

DOUGLAS BRINKLEY
WITH WINIFRED CONKLING

HARPER

An Imprint of HarperCollins*Publishers*

American Moonshot Young Readers' Edition: John F. Kennedy and the Great Space Race

Text copyright © 2019 by Douglas Brinkley

www.harpercollinschildrens.com

Library of Congress Control Number: 2018968288

ISBN 978-0-06-266028-2

Typography by Torborg Davern

19 20 21 22 23   PC/LSCH   10 9 8 7 6 5 4 3 2 1

❖

First Edition

For my daughters,
Benton Grace Brinkley and
Cassady Anne Brinkley

Both angels of pure future

Contents

PART III: MOONBOUND

PART IV: PROJECTS GEMINI AND APOLLO

AMERICAN MOONSHOT

Part I
ROCKETS

chapter one

The New Ocean

"The most difficult thing is the decision to act.
The rest is merely tenacity."
—AMELIA EARHART

On July 20, 1969, more than a half billion TV viewers watched spellbound as Apollo 11 astronaut Neil Armstrong descended from the lunar module Eagle and stepped onto the surface of the moon. It was the culmination of a journey that had begun with a presidential pledge eight years earlier, and captivated the world's imagination. Now, over the course of two hundred hours between the mission's liftoff in Florida and its splashdown in the Pacific, people were captivated by scenes of

CBS News anchor Walter Cronkite holds the *New York Times* during the Apollo 11 telecast, July 20, 1969, at 10:11 p.m.

astronauts planting the American flag on the moon's surface, bouncing in the low gravity of the lunarscape, taking photographs, and procuring moon rocks for later study back on Earth.

That first trip to the moon changed all who watched it unfold or lived in its wake. For some people, seeing images of the Earth from 238,900 miles away proved to be an almost religious experience, making them see the universe from a new perspective. The mission also redefined human limits: If

Americans could reach the moon, anything seemed possible. Maybe someday humans would also explore the inner planets Mercury, Venus, and Mars.

For Armstrong, the story of the American moonshot wasn't simply about the desire to walk on the moon. Instead, it was about duty, honor, and the patriotic determination to fulfill a bold pledge made by President John F. Kennedy on May 25, 1961. On that afternoon, the thirty-fifth president proclaimed to a joint session of Congress, "I believe that this nation should commit itself to achieving the goal, before the decade is out, of landing a man on the moon and returning him safely to Earth."

Kennedy was the only politician with the boldness and vision to risk America's international reputation on such a wild-eyed feat, and to suggest it could be done in such a short time frame. Even Kennedy's national security advisor, McGeorge Bundy, thought the idea was scientifically reckless, politically risky, and a grandstanding play of the most outlandish kind. When he told this to the president, Kennedy said, "You don't run for president in your forties unless you have a certain moxie."

Without Kennedy's leadership and insistence, the moonshot probably wouldn't have happened in 1969. The grand idea was inspired by a number of forces and factors going back to World War II and its aftermath, including new developments in rocketry, the United States' tense "Cold War" rivalry with the Soviet Union, the invention of the computer microchip, and Soviet developments in atomic bombs, intercontinental ballistic missiles, and satellite technology. Kennedy himself also had personal motivation for aiming so high, including the inspiration of a father who pushed him to achieve great things and the example of a brother who died in World War II while trying to destroy a Nazi rocket facility.

In the three and a half years before Kennedy's pledge, the Soviet Union had shocked the world, first in October 1957 by launching Sputnik, the world's first orbital satellite, and then in April 1961 by completing the first manned mission to space. The world was locked in a stalemate between rival superpowers—the United States and its democratic and capitalist system on the one side versus the Soviet Union and its communist system on the other—that became known as the Cold War. With both nations engaged in threats, propaganda, and other hostilities that stopped just short of open warfare, space inevitably became a new battlefield of competition, a place where they could prove their way was better. "Both the Soviet Union and the United States believed that technological leadership was the key to demonstrating ideological superiority," Armstrong wrote decades later. "Each invested enormous resources in evermore spectacular space achievements."

But Kennedy's Apollo moonshot plan was more than just a reaction to Soviet successes in space. It was a reassertion of America's bold spirit and a change from what he saw as the weakness of the administration of the previous two-term president, Dwight Eisenhower. Within months of winning the presidency in November 1960, Kennedy had decided that America should stop dillydallying in space. According to Kennedy's policy advisor and speechwriter Theodore Sorensen, "the lack of effort, the lack of initiative, the lack of imagination, vitality, and vision" he saw in the previous administration annoyed Kennedy to no end.

In the early 1960s, America was going through a generational shift. Only forty-three years old when he entered the White House, Kennedy was the youngest person ever elected president. The Eisenhower administration was led by a World War II hero and seemed defined by that past, while Kennedy embodied the future—a "New Frontier" in which landing on the moon was a real possibility. The new president believed in adventure, global prestige, American exceptionalism, and the power of technology. For Kennedy, space exploration continued the grand tradition of American aerospace creativity and engineering know-how, a history that included inventions like electric light, telephones, airplanes, automobiles, and atomic power.

Exploring space wouldn't be cheap. It meant pumping huge amounts of money into the National Aeronautics and Space Administration (NASA), founded in 1958, which would be leading the mission. Due to Kennedy's space initiatives, over 4 percent of the federal budget went to NASA in the mid-1960s. Notwithstanding that high financial price tag, Kennedy knew the taxpayers' investment in space would pay off in technological innovation and economic growth. The cost of Project Apollo eventually exceeded $25 billion (around $180 billion in today's dollars), but it also jump-started the technology-based economy the United States still enjoys today. Innovations developed for the space program—including global positioning systems (GPS), satellite communications, solar panels, biomedical equipment, water-purification systems, global search-and-rescue systems, freeze-drying methods for preserving food, and new ways to dispose of toxic and radioactive waste—earned back their initial expense many times over. The cost of going to the moon was enormous, but so were the benefits.

Racing the Soviets to reach the moon first was the boldest thing Kennedy did in politics. "We choose to go to the moon in this decade and do the other things, not because they are easy, but because they are hard," Kennedy said in September 1962 at Rice University. "Because that goal will serve to organize and measure the best of our energies and skills, because that challenge is one that we are willing to accept, one we are unwilling to postpone, and one which we intend to win." Kennedy had a romantic streak when it came to exploration. The president once wrote that his yearning to understand space began in his boyhood, when he spent time sailing off the New England coast, watching the stars and feeling the gravitational push and pull between the moon and tides. For the young president, space was the next step, a "New Ocean" of galactic possibility just waiting for explorers brave enough to make the journey. "We set sail on this new sea," he said, "because there is new knowledge to be gained, and new rights to be won, and they must be won and used for the progress of all people."

Kennedy's words inspired the nation in the early 1960s.

"The eyes of the world now look into space," he said, "to the moon and to the planets beyond, and we have vowed that we shall not see it governed by a hostile flag of conquest, but by a banner of freedom and peace. We have vowed that we shall not see space filled with weapons of mass destruction, but with instruments of knowledge and understanding. Yet the vows of

A new era in human history began on July 20, 1969, when Apollo 11 astronauts Neil Armstrong and Edwin "Buzz" Aldrin walked on the moon. No longer were global citizens shackled to Earth. It was John F. Kennedy's vision for an American moonshot that jump-started this epic NASA feat. Photos of moon-prints became popular in newspapers around the world.

this Nation can only be fulfilled if we in this Nation are first, and, therefore, we intend to be first."

Unfortunately, Kennedy didn't live to see the historic summer day in 1969 when we reached the moon, but what he had envisioned was a world order in which America's bold space leadership unified people and left the Cold War behind. As Kennedy had dreamed, the first human footprints on the moon were imprinted by intrepid American space travelers. Those footprints remain there to this day, protected by the moon's lack of atmosphere, wind, and water. And they will remain stamped there for time immemorial as a symbol of John F. Kennedy's New Frontier legacy. For as the Apollo 11 plaque astronauts Neil Armstrong and Buzz Aldrin left at their lunar landing site reads:

HERE MEN FROM THE PLANET EARTH
FIRST SET FOOT UPON THE MOON
JULY 1969, A.D.
WE CAME IN PEACE FOR ALL MANKIND

chapter two

Reaching beyond the Sky

History has taught us that artists are often decades ahead of engineers and scientists in imagining the future, and so it was with the idea of going to the moon. The earliest fictional account of a visit to the moon was written about 170 A.D. by Lucian of Samosata. People had no doubt been dreaming of going to the moon for thousands of years before that. More than 1,700 years later, French author Jules Verne published *From the Earth to the Moon* (1865), a fictional story of three astronauts who are shot from a gigantic cannon in Tampa, Florida, and land on the moon. The book became a bestseller and, along with its sequel, *Around the Moon*, inspired readers to reimagine what was possible.

Verne got a lot of things right in his stories. Although he was writing around the time of the American Civil War, he predicted that the United States would beat Russia, France, Great Britain, and Germany to the moon. He imagined that the spaceship would launch from the Florida coast, take four days to reach its destination, and return to Earth by splashing down in the ocean. Some of his ideas were eerily close to what actually happened in 1969.

The novels reflected the optimistic spirit of their time, when the potential for industrial and technological progress seemed limitless. This spirit of accomplishment was still alive in the early decades of the twentieth century when John Fitzgerald "Jack" Kennedy was born on May 29, 1917, in Brookline, Massachusetts, near Boston. His parents, Joe and Rose Kennedy, both grandchildren of Irish immigrants, came from families that had thrived in business and politics. Rose's father, John Fitzgerald, was a former Massachusetts congressman and mayor of Boston. Joe's parents had established themselves in business and developed political connections in the Democratic Party.

Jack was the second of what would become nine children. His family was wealthy, but money could not protect him from contracting a potentially deadly case of scarlet fever at age two. His temperature reached 104 degrees and blisters covered his body. For three weeks, his parents went to church every day to pray for his survival. Jack ultimately recovered, but he suffered from a number of serious medical problems throughout his life.

As a child, one of Jack's passions was reading books by Jules

Verne, Mark Twain, Robert Louis Stevenson, and other authors of world history and high-risk adventure. The stories of King Arthur and the Knights of the Round Table were his favorites. When not reading, he loved spending time on Massachusetts's Cape Cod seashore, and he learned to pilot sailboats in the Atlantic Ocean at an early age. His parents also instilled in Jack an appreciation for politics and global affairs. Dinnertime conversations often dealt with the week's news from the *New York Times* and the *Saturday Evening Post*, including the latest developments in aviation.

By the time Jack entered school, America had begun to develop an interest in outer space. Schools began teaching about the solar system, and local planetariums appeared from coast to coast. In the early 1920s, astronomer Edwin Hubble was observing the solar system through the Hooker Telescope, the world's largest at the time. By 1924, Hubble's findings would shatter the idea that the Milky Way encompassed the entire cosmos, instead proving that it was just one among billions of galaxies in an unimaginably vast universe.

The skies had opened up to human beings just twenty years earlier, when the Wright Brothers achieved mankind's first powered flight at Kitty Hawk, North Carolina, on December 17, 1903. Once man could fly, the idea of space flight didn't seem unattainable. Space was talked about as a new frontier to be conquered by rocket ships. News broadcasts regularly reported on advances in technology, and astronomers speculated about life in other galaxies. This interest in space went beyond party politics or regionalism. It seemed that everyone had their eyes on the skies.

In 1915, with World War I raging in Europe, the newspapers filled with grim stories about mustard gas, armored tanks, and trench warfare, the U.S. Congress created the National Advisory Committee for Aeronautics (NACA) to "supervise and direct the scientific study of the problems of flight to their practical solution," with the goal of producing cutting-edge military aircraft.

Coordinating aeronautical innovation across government, industry, and academia, the committee became the United States' first civilian aeronautical research laboratory. In 1917, the year that Jack Kennedy was born, NACA established the Langley Aeronautical Laboratory in Hampton, Virginia, situated on the Little Back River off the Chesapeake Bay, at the end of a peninsula running between the James and York Rivers. Soon the laboratory was conducting research in aerodynamics, aircraft design, and propulsion systems for both industrial and military clients. Decades later, it was at this facility that the idea of launching Americans to the moon got its first serious discussion. In 1958, NACA was reestablished as the National Aeronautics and Space Administration (NASA) by President Dwight Eisenhower and the government's focus shifted from the skies to the stars.

When Jack Kennedy was just a boy, the theoretical foundations of America's space program were being laid less than forty-five miles from his Brookline home, in Worcester, Massachusetts. There, Dr. Robert H. Goddard, a professor at Clark College (now Clark University), published a seventy-nine-page book titled *A Method of Reaching Extreme Altitudes*, which explained the principles of constructing a two-stage, solid-propellant rocket for use in atmospheric research. The most exciting part of the research was Goddard's bold claim that this kind of rocket would allow objects to reach beyond the Earth's atmosphere.

As early as 1912, Goddard had become the first credible American to explore mathematically the idea of adopting rocket propulsion to reach high altitudes. Hoping to someday make money on his ideas, Goddard applied for patents, eventually receiving over two hundred of them, including the first for a multistage rocket. During World War I, Goddard worked with the U.S. Army, developing a tube-based rocket launcher that later became the bazooka, a light infantry weapon widely used in World War II.

Goddard was an academic, but he wanted to build and launch his own rockets to prove his newfangled theories. He argued that Isaac Newton's third law of motion—for every action, there is an equal and opposite reaction—applies to motion in space just like it does on Earth.

His ideas were discussed in newspapers across the country, but not always favorably. The *New York Times* said Goddard "lacked the knowledge ladled out daily in high schools," arguing that his rocket would not perform in space because it would have no atmosphere to push against.

Other aeronautical engineers supported Goddard's argument that a rocket could function in a vacuum, and Goddard soon found a way to prove his case. Speaking before an assembly of his students, he rigged a .22-caliber pistol atop a revolving spindle, loaded it with a blank cartridge, inserted it into a glass container, then drew out all the air from the container to simulate the vacuum of outer space. When he fired the gun electronically, it kicked back and made four revolutions inside the jar, dramatically showing thrust and velocity. Goddard concluded by saying, "So much for the *New York Times*." More than fifty other experiments proved that rocket propulsion would work in the void of outer space.

By 1921, Goddard was convinced that he could achieve greater thrust in his rockets by switching from solid fuel (such as gunpowder) to liquid fuel (such as gasoline and liquid oxygen). To test his ideas, he needed money. In an effort to raise funds, he promoted the idea that he was designing a rocket that could reach the moon. He teased the public imagination, announcing that he had received nine applications from fearless men who wanted to soar to the moon in the first rocket. Of course, he was not actually planning to send a rocket to the moon, but that didn't matter. Across the country, people imagined a moon launch, and people asked one another: Would you go?

In the early 1920s, Goddard's experiments generated excitement not only in the United States but also in Germany, where Hermann Oberth, a German national born in Romania, was working on similar ideas. Like Goddard, Oberth had been fascinated with the idea of space travel since reading Verne's *From the Earth to the Moon*. Oberth reached out to Goddard, and the two scientists began a friendly correspondence. In 1923, Oberth published a book claiming that liquid-propelled rockets could escape the Earth's atmosphere, making interplanetary travel possible.

Oberth's book soon reached the young Soviet Union, which had only come into being in 1922, in the long wake of 1917's Russian Revolution. While the country was still largely closed off from the Western world, news of Goddard's and Oberth's research in space exploration found its way in, and the two scientists became heroes to university scientists and the Soviet people in general. This newfound enthusiasm for rocketry also helped rescue the career of the Soviet Union's own rocket genius, Konstantin Tsiolkovsky, who had written similarly about rockets in papers and books but had gotten little acclaim.

Back in Germany, someone who would eventually play a huge part in the development of space rocketry was still a bookish young boy who played piano and dreamed of becoming a composer. Born on March 23, 1912, Wernher von Braun became fascinated by the stars and rocketry at age twelve. Having read about automobiles powered by rockets, Wernher built a contraption using a wagon with six large firework skyrockets fastened to the back. He lit the fuse on a public street and the rockets took off, completely out of control and trailing a comet's tail of fire. Fortunately, no one was injured, but even though he was briefly taken into custody by the police for his stunt, von Braun was ecstatic. It was the beginning of a lifetime of rocketry experiments.

In the United States, Goddard's promised launch of the first liquid-fueled rocket had been repeatedly postponed. Finally, on March 16, 1926, Goddard and two assistants gathered on a snowy cabbage field in Auburn, Massachusetts, to conduct the experiment. Goddard mixed liquid oxygen with gasoline in the rocket's combustion chamber, and his friend used a blowtorch to touch off the black-powder igniter. The ten-foot-tall rocket lifted into the sky, reaching an altitude of forty-one feet in two seconds, averaging sixty miles per hour, before crashing back to Earth.

The experiment was a success. No one could deny the viability of liquid-fueled propulsion, which provided greater thrust than gunpowder while allowing greater control over how long the rockets burned. He continued with his experiments, leading up to his ambitious test of the world's first multistage rocket on July 17, 1929. This test involved a larger version of his early designs, with a series of liquid-fuel compartments designed to go off in succession. It also carried a barometer, a thermometer, and a camera.

This time, when his team lit the fuse, the rocket released a series of sonic roars that could be heard two miles away as the rocket shot ninety feet in the air. When neighbors looked up,

Robert H. Goddard poses with a liquid-fueled rocket contraption on March 16, 1926, in Worcester, Massachusetts. Although this rocket rose only forty-one feet, Goddard's immense body of work, covered by 214 patents, established him as one of the founders of spaceflight.

they saw something falling to Earth and thought a pilot had fallen out of an airplane. They called for ambulances, police cars, and a search plane to assist with the disaster. When the residents learned that Goddard had been conducting his experiment, they forbade him from ever launching another rocket inside city limits, forcing him to find another launch site.

In Germany, Professor Hermann Oberth wasn't faring much better. He had a hard time raising money for academic research, so he agreed to look to private sources of funding. In 1928 he had been hired by a movie director to build a working rocket that would be launched as publicity for the film's premiere. The rocket wasn't ready by showtime, so he didn't get any additional financial support from the company.

In 1930, Oberth befriended a new student at the Technische Hochschule Berlin (Technical University of Berlin): Wernher von Braun, the young man with the wagon rocket. On a couple of occasions, von Braun began helping the older scientist with his innovative rocket experiments and also worked as a fundraiser for their research. For a time, one of von Braun's responsibilities was to spend eight hours a day manning a display on space exploration at a Berlin department store, asking for money. As part of his pitch, von Braun would say, "I bet you that the first man to walk on the moon is alive today somewhere on this Earth!" As it turned out, he was right: That very year, future moonwalker Neil Armstrong was born on a farm outside of the small town of Wapakoneta, Ohio.

In the United States, Goddard was also desperate for

funding. Fortunately for him, he was approached by the famous Minnesota aviator Charles Lindbergh, who was interested in the idea of rocket-powered planes. Just two years before, in May 1927, Lindbergh had become the first aviator to fly solo nonstop across the Atlantic aboard his plane *Spirit of St. Louis*, a feat that had turned him into a worldwide celebrity. After meeting with Goddard, Lindbergh convinced New York philanthropist Daniel Guggenheim to support his theoretical research and experiments. Through his Guggenheim Fund for the Promotion of Aeronautics, Guggenheim offered Goddard $100,000 (almost $1.5 million in today's dollars), in payments divided over four years. With this funding in place, Goddard moved his rocket experiments to Roswell, New Mexico. It was an ideal site for his work, a desertscape offering flat and dry terrain, uncloudy weather, and a sparse population. Experimenting with rockets in a crowded town or city would just have been too dangerous.

Out in the desert, away from the public glare, Goddard made steady progress. In the spring of 1937, he launched a rocket that reached an altitude of nearly 9,000 feet in just 22.3 seconds. Even as Goddard worked as America's only serious rocket experimenter, the field of rocketry was moving in a more threatening direction on the other side of the globe, as Europe was edging ever closer to another world war.

chapter three

Rocketing into Battle

As the 1930s began, John F. Kennedy was twelve years old and living in Westchester County, New York. Both his father and mother traveled often, sometimes staying away for months at a time. Jack looked to his older brother, Joseph Jr., as a role model for all that he did—and did not—want to become. Joe was smart and driven and he seemed to be born for greatness. But he could also be bullying and quick-tempered, especially when under pressure.

In late October 1929, the U.S. stock market crashed, ushering in the Great Depression, an era of widespread bank failures, job losses, and poverty. Jack's family continued to live in luxury, but his parents didn't want their son to be soft and feel entitled, so they pushed him to be as tough and resilient as his older brother. Jack was burdened with high expectations, but he almost always met the demands with confidence and good cheer.

When Jack was eleven years old, a story by writer Philip Francis Nowlan appeared in *Amazing Stories* magazine, detailing the adventures of an American World War I hero who falls into suspended animation and wakes up five hundred years in the future. Soon adapted into a daily newspaper cartoon and then a radio show, Buck Rogers became wildly popular among boys and girls, who avidly followed his adventures fighting Martians, outer-space pirates, and other evil invaders. Building on the craze, newspapers launched other science fiction comics. One of the most popular was *Flash Gordon*, which featured interplanetary travel in rockets. These comics—forerunners of today's Marvel superheroes—encouraged Kennedy's generation to consider space as the next frontier for exploration.

In the summer of 1930, Jack went to boarding school at Canterbury, in New Milford, Connecticut. While there he suffered from an attack of appendicitis, but he didn't complain. Like his father, Jack considered his gripes a bore to others, so he kept his pains to himself as much as possible. The following year, Jack transferred to Choate, another elite Connecticut boarding school. Again, he suffered several bouts of illness. In 1934 he was struck with a digestive disorder that caused fatigue, weight loss, and pain. He spent the spring semester in a hospital room, and his recovery took most of the year.

As a student, Jack proved to be popular but unfocused. "Jack has rather superior mental ability without the deep interest in his studies or the mature viewpoint that demands of him his best effort all the time," wrote the Choate headmaster of Jack's performance at age eighteen. "We have been and are working our hardest to develop Jack's own self-interest . . . to the point that will assure him a record in college more worthy of his natural gifts of intelligence, likeability, and popularity."

After graduation, Kennedy began his college career at Princeton, but illness forced him to withdraw during his first semester. When he recovered, he applied to and was accepted at Harvard. He started classes there in 1936, and by his junior year he had focused his studies on government, political science, and foreign relations. Still, he didn't take himself too seriously. He often flew to New York City for weekends filled with parties and nightclubs. He also visited his family home in Hyannis Port on the Cape Cod peninsula, where he had a good time with wealthy friends from nearby towns.

Like Kennedy, Wernher von Braun attended elite boarding schools before beginning college at the Technical University of Berlin. Every year, his overriding passion for rocketry grew. In one important regard, however, he differed from his hero, Professor Oberth. Von Braun supported the militarization of rocketry by the German government, while Oberth did not.

In January 1933, Adolf Hitler was appointed chancellor of Germany and quickly gained power. Von Braun saw cooperation with the military as the best path to securing funding for rocket research, so he entered the Nazi Party's new, well-funded rocket program. On December 18, 1932, von Braun launched two advanced A-2 rockets to altitudes of 6,500 feet. Based on that success, the twenty-two-year-old was granted funding to build bigger and better rockets.

By the late 1930s, global events were setting the stage for a battle between democracy and fascism, a form of government characterized by an authoritarian dictator who suppresses opposition and promotes national identity above individual rights. Recognizing that the United States might soon be drawn into the brewing European conflict, Robert Goddard tried to convince top generals and admirals in the American military to develop long-range rockets to be used as weapons.

Most of America's military leaders weren't interested, but Major Jimmy Doolittle was the exception. Doolittle had become fascinated in space science as a boy. During World War I, he was an accomplished Army Air Corps pilot. After the war, he became a master of aeronautical technology, helping to develop new flight instruments that let pilots navigate through dense fog, cloud banks, darkness, and thunderstorms. He also studied how a pilot's hearing and vision were affected by high altitudes. In the 1930s, he shattered a number of aviation speed records.

In October 1938, Doolittle briefly went to New Mexico to study rocket propulsion with Goddard. Doolittle recognized the possible importance of rockets in warfare.

In the summer of 1937, before his sophomore year at Harvard, Jack Kennedy traveled through England, France, Italy, Austria,

Germany, and the Netherlands with a school friend. In part, Jack made the trip so he could see firsthand how Hitler was transforming Germany, and make his own judgments. He spent time talking to local people, trying to learn what life was like for them. At the time, Germany was forming military pacts with Italy and Japan. The Dachau concentration camp was in operation. Jews had been segregated and stripped of their rights, and Roma people, Slavs, Jehovah's Witnesses, and homosexuals, among others, also faced persecution.

Despite newspaper reports on the human rights abuses of Hitler's fascist government and the militarism that fueled German economic growth, some wealthy American and British families admired the Nazis. Many American intellectuals and corporate leaders mistakenly believed that Hitler's rule had led to efficiencies in business and to social stability. Jack Kennedy's father and older brother appreciated Germany as a pro-business nation. Joe Jr. thought that Germany had bested the United States in railways, aviation, medicine, forestry, and engineering.

At the time, U.S. political leaders were divided between internationalists and isolationists: those who thought America should take a stand on global affairs and those who thought it best to mind our own business. President Franklin D. Roosevelt wanted to be militarily ready for a fascist threat to European and American democracy, but he had to move slowly. The isolationists were a powerful and well-organized group. Some wanted to avoid the conflict because they remembered the horrors of World War I, while others actually thought German domination of Europe might have some advantages.

In March 1938, Roosevelt appointed Jack's father, Joseph Kennedy Sr., as ambassador to the Court of St. James, the royal court of the United Kingdom. That summer, Jack returned to Europe, this time with his brother Joe Jr. They stayed and worked at the American embassy in London. While working unofficially on minor assignments at the embassy, Jack traveled to the Soviet Union, Germany, and Poland, impressing his colleagues with his deep knowledge of world history.

Back at Harvard in the fall, Jack studied global affairs. At first, he argued in favor of American isolation, writing an unsigned Harvard newspaper editorial titled "Peace in Our Time," which urged the United States and Britain not to engage in hostilities in Europe. But the more he studied the Third Reich while writing his honors thesis, the more Kennedy realized Hitler was a monster who had to be stopped.

In June 1940, Jack graduated cum laude (with distinction) from Harvard, earning a bachelor's degree. Later that year, his thesis was published as a bestselling book, *Why England Slept*. Jack continued to edge away from his father's politics, becoming increasingly convinced that the United States needed to take a military stand against Hitler and the growing fascist threat in Europe.

Military technology was a priority for the Nazi regime, but the Germans kept quiet about their innovations and research.

Future American president John F. Kennedy sits at a typewriter in 1940, holding open his published Harvard thesis, *Why England Slept.*

After World War I, several nations had been trying to develop the first jet airplane. Italy thought it won with its first design in 1940, not realizing that a German Heinkel jet had already been flying for a year.

The Germans kept their rocket development secret, too. German engineers were quietly designing a military liquid-fueled rocket that could be mass-produced and extend the range of traditional artillery. The German rocket program was headed by Dr. Walter Dornberger, assisted by Wernher von Braun and several others. Dornberger was impressed by von Braun's energy, shrewdness, and "astonishing theoretical knowledge." Soon, von Braun was leading Dornberger's research team at the Kummersdorf test range, miles from South Berlin, developing and testing the first of his Aggregat series of rockets, the A-1 and A-2.

By the mid-1930s, this rocket program had attracted the support of Nazi Germany's new air force, but other military officers showed less interest. In 1936, the head of the Research and Development Department of the German Army's Board of Ordnance gave Dornberger some advice: "If you want more money, you have to prove that your rocket is of military value."

The rocket engineers took that advice, focusing their efforts on developing a game-changing ballistic missile. Their blueprints were based on a giant German howitzer used against Paris at the end of World War I. Then the longest-range artillery weapon known, it was capable of lobbing a shell weighing more than 1,000 pounds to a target eight miles away. Dornberger and von Braun's new rocket would carry nearly a hundred times more explosives than that howitzer, be capable of twice the range, and, with an accuracy of .3 percent of its range, it could actually hit its target. In addition, the rocket's length would be less than forty-two feet, so it could be transported in a single piece by truck or railroad car.

The German military authorized the development of the rocket. To ensure secrecy, the Third Reich established a top secret war rocket facility at Usedom, a remote island on the coast of the Baltic Sea, south of Sweden. Christened Peenemünde after a small fishing village there, it began operation in 1937 and soon became the most modern ballistic missile development facility in the world, with a staff of about three hundred.

Despite the size and sophistication of the Peenemünde effort, few people yet knew of the effort to turn rockets into long-range military weapons. Even within the German Army, the site's mission was kept hush-hush, but it was a hive of activity. In addition to rockets, the facility was developing a winged guided missile known as the Vergeltungswaffe 1 ("Vengeance Weapon 1"), or V-1 for short. Between 1937 and 1941, von Braun launched more than seventy Aggregat rockets there, including the Vergeltungswaffe 2, which would become known to the world as the V-2.

While the rocket research was being conducted for military purposes, von Braun was always mindful of the technology's potential for space exploration. In one discussion, von Braun

A V-2 rocket in launching position at Peenemünde (German Army Research Center) during World War II.

interrupted a presentation about armed rockets to talk about breaking gravity's hold on mankind and going to the moon. Von

Braun was shut down, imprisoned for two weeks, and sternly told never to speak about space travel in front of other officers. He was ordered to focus his energies on long-range plotting for the Third Reich to control Europe. His rockets were to be used to destroy cities like London, England, and Antwerp, Belgium, not to go to the moon.

Hitler wasn't interested in space research, believing the cosmos hopelessly dull and remote. But he did want his rocket-powered ballistic missiles. While the research team hoped to have a working liquid-fueled weapon ready by 1943, that seemed like an intolerable delay to Hitler, who was rapidly gearing up for war. In September 1939, German forces invaded neighboring Poland. In response, Britain declared war on Germany. World War II was on, and in response Dornberger and von Braun pushed their team to have their rocket ready faster.

In the fall of 1940, Jack Kennedy began taking graduate classes in business, economics, and political science at Stanford University. He carefully followed global events and strongly supported American involvement in the war. That summer, most of the European continent fell to the Nazis and only Britain remained free. From August to October 1940, the German air force unleashed wave after wave of bombers in a campaign against British towns, cities, shipping, airfields, and radar bases.

Hitler had assumed his air force could destroy Britain's Royal Air Force, paving the way for British surrender and an invasion by German troops. What Hitler didn't count on was that the British and their airmen grew tougher, not weaker, in the face of the relentless attacks. Hitler shifted his focus from attacks on the air force to attacks on civilian targets in London. The proud and defiant British refused to break. The Blitz, as the campaign was known, just strengthened the British resolve to defeat the Germans.

Frustrated that his assault against Britain wasn't causing its surrender, Hitler turned to the east, attacking the Soviet Union in June 1941 with a lightning-fast blitzkrieg attack. Involving more than three and a half million German, Finnish, and Romanian troops and 3,500 tanks, it was the largest invasion force in history. The Soviet losses were so devastating that Hitler regained confidence and decided to renew his aerial attack against the British.

With these extensive military campaigns going on, there were fewer resources available for ballistic missle development. In this make-or-break moment, Colonel Dornberger and von Braun tried to persuade the Führer to continue supporting their work by touting its effect as a psychological weapon that could break the spirit of the British people. In a meeting with Hitler on August 20, 1941, Dornberger and von Braun described their rocket traveling at 3,500 miles per hour, appearing seemingly from nowhere. By the time anyone on the ground saw it coming, they would have only seconds before it would slam 4,000 pounds of explosives into a crowded London neighborhood, destroying blocks in every direction. In addition, they promised they could develop rockets with stabilizing wings and two-stage propulsions, which would be able to perhaps reach the shores of the United States in a few years' time.

Hitler considered the proposal, which appealed to his grandiose sense of his own power and Germany's technological superiority, and decided to give Dornberger and von Braun the resources to make it happen.

In 1941, no other nation had Germany's momentum in the field of rocketry, partly because Hitler's diabolical drive for world domination meant he was willing to put vast resources into developing rockets as weapons. He came to believe von Braun's rockets would change the course of the war, and in fact they did—but not in the way he intended. According to Nazi officers at the time and military historians since, Hitler's commitment to the V-2 actually decreased Germany's chances of winning the war by draining resources that could have been used to build more conventional weapons and aircraft.

Ironically, though, Hitler's commitment to von Braun's V-2 ultimately helped rocketry achieve a goal Goddard, Oberth, and von Braun himself had long dreamed of: going to space. Though Hitler may have had no interest in space research, the advances made under his missile program pushed rocket science forward by leaps and bounds, heavily influencing the technology the U.S. government would use in the 1950s and 1960s to go to space—and then to the moon.

chapter four

Racing against the Third Reich

J ack Kennedy knew all about sailing, but he didn't always play by the rules. He longed to test himself against the elements. The fiercer the wind, the more exhilarated he became. Some called his extreme sailing reckless or said he had a death wish, but Kennedy didn't care. He felt most authentic—his truest self—when he was near the ocean.

With his love of all things nautical, it came as no surprise that Kennedy chose the U.S. Navy when he decided to join the military. On September 25, 1941, at age twenty-four, he was sworn in as an ensign, the lowest rank of naval commissioned officer. Jack's older brother, Joe Jr., had taken a break from Harvard Law School and joined the Naval Reserve to train as a pilot during the second half of 1941, earning his naval wings in March 1942. Joe Jr. held lofty ideas about duty and devotion to America, and he believed there was nothing he couldn't achieve through focus, drive, and hard work. He never expressed any direct desire to be a senator or governor, but a sense of political destiny swirled around him.

Portrait of Ensign Joseph P. Kennedy Jr. (right) and Lieutenant (junior grade) John F. Kennedy in their Navy uniforms. The photograph was taken in May 1942 by Turgeon Studios.

With the U.S. by now providing ships, planes, and weaponry to help the British resist Hitler, both brothers were fully committed to the effort. They never tried to use their father's influence to avoid military service, and were ready to fight if the United States declared war. Then, just ten weeks after Jack's commission, it happened. Taking the U.S. completely by surprise, the forces of the Japanese Empire bombed the U.S. Navy base at Pearl Harbor in Hawaii on the morning of December 7, sinking four battleships, heavily damaging many other vessels, destroying 188 aircraft, and killing 2,403 Americans. The next day, President Roosevelt called it "a date which will live in infamy" and led Congress to declare war on Japan. Three days later, on December 11, 1941, Nazi Germany and its Axis partners declared war on the United States. Jack and Joe Kennedy Jr. were already in uniform and ready to serve.

The United States joined the Allied forces—Great Britain, Australia, and the Soviet Union, among other countries—in fighting against the Axis: Germany, Italy, and Japan. Almost immediately, U.S. factories switched from making consumer goods to producing military supplies. Soldiers enlisted to do their part. Between 1940 and 1943, enlistment in the U.S. Armed Forces expanded from fewer than 500,000 to more than 9 million.

At first, it appeared that Jack Kennedy was headed for service at the Office of Naval Intelligence in Washington. With his health problems and background as a bestselling author, a desk job focused on researching and writing reports seemed ideal.

But Jack wanted a naval combat role in the Pacific, fighting against Japan.

While Jack Kennedy was adjusting to Navy life, rocket scientist Wernher von Braun joined the Nazi Party and became an officer in the Allgemeine SS, a major branch of the Schutzstaffel ("Protection Squadron"). Operated by Adolf Hitler and the Nazi Party, the SS was a paramilitary organization dedicated to enforcing the Reich's racist laws, running its concentration and extermination camps, seeking out and crushing political dissent, and working with the German military. Von Braun later argued he had no choice in joining, but his critics point out that many of his colleagues found ways to resist the fascist regime and its evil policies, which would ultimately lead to the murder of six million Jews and countless others the Reich considered "undesirable."

The demands of the German rocket program were becoming intense. Von Braun typically slept only four hours a day. Hitler set the goal of producing 5,000 V-2 rockets a year. Von Braun didn't think it was possible, but he didn't dare speak out. At that point, a practical version of the V-2 had yet to be tested.

Von Braun was a perfectionist. He wanted to refine the V-2, but time was running out. He launched the first official V-2 test rocket in July 1942. It reached a very low altitude, and then blew up. Von Braun worked out the kinks, and in a follow-up test a month later, the V-2 reached an impressive altitude of seven miles before falling apart.

The rocket was improving steadily. In October 1942, a V-2 broke the sound barrier, traveling to an altitude of fifty-two and a half miles and pushing into the ionosphere, the band of thin air that separates the Earth's atmosphere from outer space. This test marked the first time a man-made object had ever flown that close to escaping the Earth's atmosphere. If such a rocket could be weaponized and mass produced quickly, Nazi Germany might prove unbeatable.

While von Braun worked on perfecting his rocket, U.S. and British troops landed at several locations in French North Africa. They met with little resistance and made their way north to the western border of Tunisia. With the Allies threatening to push into Europe, Hitler decided the V-2 was essential to victory, and pushed the V-2 engineers at Peenemünde even harder.

As the Allies made progress in North Africa, Jack Kennedy completed Officer Training School at Northwestern University in Chicago. On October 10, 1942, he attained the rank of lieutenant, junior grade, and immediately volunteered for Patrol Torpedo (PT) boat service in the Pacific. PT boats were long and fast, with a top speed of forty knots (just over forty-six miles per hour). They were heavily armed and designed to interrupt enemy supply lines by sinking barges, freighters, and sometimes warships. Because they attacked their Japanese targets in buzzing swarms, PTs were known as "mosquito boats" to American sailors.

Looking like enlarged, fortified racing speedboats, PT boats carried two officers and a crew of eleven. When selecting the officers, the Navy looked for graduates of first-rate colleges, preferably men who had played on team sports. Higher priority was given to men who knew how to sail. Because the assignment was extremely dangerous, the Navy also preferred men who weren't married.

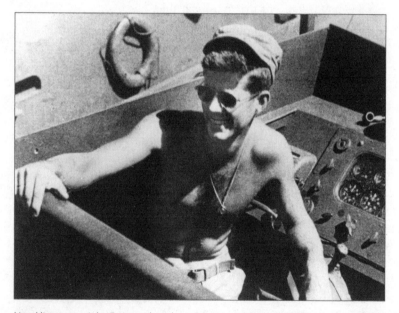

Naval lieutenant John F. Kennedy on board the torpedo boat PT-109 he commanded in the southwest Pacific.

In March 1943, Kennedy was given command of PT-109 as a lieutenant. He took command on April 23 and was ordered to the Solomon Islands. On August 2, 1943, PT-109 was moving as quietly as possible in an area where Japanese supply ships ran their routes. At about 2:00 a.m., a Japanese destroyer rammed their boat, which immediately broke apart and began sinking.

Two of his men were dead, but Kennedy remained cool-headed. He saved an injured sailor by pulling him through shark-infested waters until they found a piece of floating debris. Over the course of twelve hours, all of the survivors made it to an island three miles away. On August 8, six days after the accident, Kennedy and his surviving crew were rescued. Kennedy returned to the PT base as a naval hero and was assigned to another PT boat.

Back in Europe, American and British forces started a bombing campaign to slow Germany's rocket program. On August 17, 1943, almost six hundred bombers—one of the largest air raid forces ever assembled by the Royal Air Force—filled the skies over northeast Germany on a mission to find and attack Dornberger's and von Braun's Peenemünde facility. The attack lasted two hours and killed 733 people, including 557 prisoners and slave laborers who had been brought in to work on the assembly lines. At first it seemed that the attack had destroyed Peenemünde, but it soon became clear that the base could still operate. Missile production continued, and the bombing didn't delay the research on the V-2 in a meaningful way.

The Nazis responded by developing another rocket facility in a secret underground location carved into a remote mountain slope in Thuringia, in northern Germany.

It should have taken years to build, but the Germans

accelerated the process by using concentration camp slave labor to transform the rocky cliff into the Mittelwerk missile factory. There, with no fresh air and little water or food, slaves worked to build von Braun's V-2 rockets, and were routinely beaten and tortured for not working fast enough. Those who became sick or injured were executed by their Nazi overseers. By the end of the effort, thousands of laborers had died at the facility. Von Braun was complicit in these deaths and probably would have been charged with war crimes if he hadn't managed to strike a deal with the U.S. after it became clear Germany lost the war.

Jack Kennedy suffered a back injury during the sinking of PT-109, which ultimately led to his medical discharge from the military. In January 1944, he was asked to cooperate with a *Life* magazine article about the night of the accident. With his father's blessing, Kennedy agreed to work with the reporter, who met Kennedy in his hospital room after he had undergone back surgery.

While Kennedy was recovering in Florida, the war raged on, but the end was near. On June 6—known as D-Day—the Allies launched the largest amphibious assault in the history of the world, landing an initial force of 156,000 troops on five beaches along a fifty-mile stretch of the fortified Normandy coast, in Nazi-occupied France. The huge number of soldiers overwhelmed the Nazi defenses, allowing the Allies to gain a foothold in Europe and begin pushing the Nazis back.

The Germans continued with their relentless bombing

campaigns against Britain and other targets. Since the V-2 missiles weren't ready yet, they relied on the V-1, a far less complex weapon, which was essentially an unmanned jet plane with a simple autopilot. Between June and September 1944, more than 8,000 of these "buzz bombs" (also called "Doodlebugs" because of their characteristic engine sound) were launched against London, flying just under the speed of sound and packed with a ton of explosives. Three-quarters of them were duds, suffering from malfunctions or guidance errors, and even those that hit their targets sometimes failed to explode. Still, with more than one hundred coming in daily during the peak period of the attack, those that worked as intended caused massive destruction.

With Britain's air force fighting off V-1 attacks, the Allies focused on trying to find and destroy the underground Mittelwerk V-2 manufacturing plant. The Allies wrongly believed that the V-2 required a long pipe or cannon for launch. They thought the most likely facility was a heavily fortified cave-like compound in northeastern France. U.S. intelligence reported that the compound had a series of tunnels and underground workshops. While the facility didn't focus on V-2 production, it did house another secret German weapon: the V-3, a long-range gun that was supposed to be able to fire large-scale explosives to London at a rate of five shells per minute, twenty-four hours a day.

By mid-June 1944, the Nazis' French compound became a major target, with Allied commanders approving a daring plan to destroy it. To carry out the mission, dubbed Operation Aphrodite, the military needed experienced pilots as well as old B-17 and B-24 bombers that had seen too much action but could still be useful for one last mission.

In June 1944, Jack Kennedy became a celebrity when the *New Yorker* magazine published "Survival," an article about the sinking of PT-109. After the story's initial publication, Kennedy's father encouraged *Reader's Digest*, the country's most widely read magazine at the time, to reprint the heroic tale. He also privately published the story in pamphlet form and passed it out free of cost. Almost overnight, Jack Kennedy went from a privileged Ivy Leaguer to a bona fide World War II hero.

In August 1944, as the *Reader's Digest* article was about to appear, twenty-nine-year-old Lieutenant Joe Kennedy Jr. was in England. He had completed his twenty-fifth mission, making him eligible to return home, but instead he volunteered to fly in Operation Aphrodite. Joe learned that his plane would be going only one way: After takeoff, Joe and his copilot would put the aircraft on remote control, activate 25,000 pounds of high explosives, and then parachute out. The plane—now an airborne bomb—would then fly on remote control until it crashed into the mouth of what they believed to be Hitler's secret missile plant.

Joe Jr. and his copilot, Wilford "Bud" Willy, took off on August 12 from England. As planned, they reached the designated altitude of 2,000 feet and switched the plane to remote control. They began arming the fuses, but they never had the chance to bail out. An explosion vaporized the plane in flight, killing Kennedy and Willy instantly. A fragment of radio was the only piece of the plane ever recovered.

Two priests arrived at the Kennedy home at Hyannis Port, Massachusetts, to inform the family of Joe Jr.'s death. Over the following days, Joe's parents proudly received their son's Navy Cross and Air Medal. Joe Kennedy Sr. never learned the classified details of the mission that had killed his oldest son. Only in 1963, when Jack was president, did he learn the truth.

chapter five

Every Man for Himself

On June 20, 1944, as southern England was suffering wave after wave of V-1 attacks and Allied forces were pushing back German forces in France, Wernher von Braun conducted his most successful V-2 test to date. Blasting past the Kármán line—the boundary between Earth's atmosphere and outer space—the rocket reached an altitude of 109 miles, becoming the first man-made object in space.

Despite this success, the German military was becoming impatient with von Braun's slow progress, and on August 6, 1944, installed General Hans Kammler as the V-2 project's new director, with a mandate to speed things along. Von Braun loathed his new boss, who made unreasonable demands as he pushed to get the missile ready for action. A few weeks later, Adolf Hitler ordered the V-2 attacks to begin as soon as possible.

Rocket engineer Wernher von Braun spent the Second World War in service to Hitler's Third Reich, building V-2s to be used against France, Belgium, the Netherlands, and Great Britain. Here he is at the Army Rocket Center at Peenemünde, meeting officers of the Wehrmacht during a demonstration launch of the V-2 rocket in 1944. At the time he was technical director at the Army Rocket Center.

The Allies were hunting for launch sites, unaware that the V-2 launch device was mobile. Even though the rockets were forty-six feet in length and weighed more than thirteen tons, they were mounted on truck trailers and could be quickly towed into position and fired, making it difficult for the Allies to track their locations. On September 6, the Nazis were finally ready to launch the first V-2s at their enemies. The first rocket was launched toward Paris, which the Allies had liberated from Nazi control two weeks before. The first rocket landed near the Porte d'Italie, causing no casualties.

The following day, German soldiers ordered residents of a suburban neighborhood in The Hague, Netherlands, to leave the area. Military vehicles hauling V-2 mobile launch platforms quickly set up on the streets and launched two more V-2s, this time aimed at London. The rockets were in position within an hour, and thirty minutes later the now-empty trucks were ready to move on. One of the rockets caused only minor damage, but the others demolished part of a British suburb, killing three people.

That evening, von Braun was told of the launches on Paris and London, and reports of his reaction differ. According to one account, von Braun was devastated. "This should never have happened," he reportedly said. "I always hoped the war would be over before they launched [the V-2] against a live target. We built our rocket to pave the way to other worlds, not to raise havoc on Earth." Another colleague, though, recalled the von Braun team celebrating the successful V-2 strikes with champagne. Which version of von Braun's reaction is the truth? Perhaps both: The engineer often told people what they wanted to hear in order to keep his rocket program secure. But even if he thought of his work with the Nazis as just a means to an end—a way of advancing his research and reaching outer space—there's really no way to justify putting such powerful weapons in the hands of a lunatic like Adolf Hitler. When you make a deal with the devil, you're tainted forever by his crimes.

After the initial launch, V-2s began striking London at a rate of about two hundred per month for the next half a year. The rockets were far from perfect. Some V-2s hit their targets but failed to explode. Others burst in the air. Still, the attacks resulted in enormous damage and loss of life. All told, Germany launched more than 4,300 V-2s before the war ended the following May, killing an estimated 9,000 civilians and military personnel and injuring 25,000 more. On top of these are the many thousands of slave laborers who died producing V-2 missiles, V-1 flying bombs, and other weapons at the Mittelwerk factory. Even if von Braun wasn't directly responsible for their deaths, he was certainly complicit.

The Third Reich was being squeezed from all sides. As the Allies pushed into Europe, the Soviets closed in on Germany from the east. The war had cost the lives of an astounding 24 million Soviets, but Joseph Stalin's Red Army was still fighting.

Hitler continued to attack Britain and Belgium, his two major targets. In a final effort to avoid defeat, the Mittelwerk facility was ordered to accelerate V-2 production in early 1945, and would manufacture almost 900 V-2s per month until production stopped in February. On March 27, the last V-2 of World War II was launched.

The war was winding down. When U.S. troops crossed the Rhine River in March 1945, Hitler ordered the destruction of German infrastructure to prevent its use by the invading forces. But securing Germany's bridges, factories, and communication facilities wasn't the Americans' only aim. They also wanted to take Germany's top scientists into custody before they escaped or were captured by the Soviets. Aeronautical engineers, fuel experts, naval weaponeers, physicists, chemists, and thousands of others were on the wanted list—and one of the most important names on that list was Wernher von Braun.

On February 17, von Braun organized an evacuation of his laboratory, spiriting away his top employees as well as equipment, blueprints, and research documents in a fleet of trucks, cars, and trains. In mid-March, General Hans Kammler ordered von Braun to destroy all V-2 blueprints, production drawings, and other documents and then evacuate to the Bavarian Alps with five hundred of his key personnel. Von Braun knew these documents and mechanical parts could be valuable in negotiating favorable treatment with the Allies, so he instead hid them in a mine shaft and dynamited the entrances.

In this final phase of the war, Germany's scientists and their knowledge had become valuable assets. Von Braun decided that his safest option was to surrender to the U.S. Army. He and many of his brightest engineers escaped and hid in a resort town near the Austrian border. Days later, they learned that Hitler had committed suicide in Berlin, beginning a process that would end with Germany's unconditional surrender.

On May 2, 1945, von Braun and his rocket team surrendered to the U.S. Army, providing the United States military with the know-how, research, and technology to become the premier rocket-builder in the world. In one of the great technology grabs in world history, U.S. forces collected fourteen tons of blueprints and design drawings from von Braun's mine shaft, as well as enough parts to assemble one hundred V-2s. Three days later, Soviet forces captured von Braun's former laboratory along with its hardware and production facilities, but the most vital personnel, documents, and equipment were already in American hands.

Realizing he was in a race with the United States and was already falling behind, Soviet leader Joseph Stalin fumed. The Soviets didn't get von Braun, but they weren't left empty-handed. They claimed enough machinery and components to resume rocket production at Peenemünde before moving the captured German technicians and materials to the Soviet Union, where the V-2 began a second career as the Soviet R-1.

Von Braun was sure his technological know-how would buy

him protected status in the United States, even though his work had led to the deaths of thousands of British civilians. In the months and years after the war, many military officers who ordered the use of the V-2s on civilians were charged with war crimes, and those who fired the rockets were treated as enemy combatants. But as von Braun had predicted, the scientists who designed the weapons to maximize their lethal power were given immunity and protection as long as they were willing to surrender and work for the Americans.

At first, von Braun's team and their families were housed in southern Germany in a complex built to house athletes in the 1936 Olympics. They told their American captors that they had been forced to work for their homeland during the war. Now that Germany had been defeated, the Nazi rocket engineers conveniently switched their loyalties and agreed to help the United States become a global leader in ballistic missile manufacturing.

Within weeks of Germany's surrender, the U.S. Army began shipping V-2 rocket parts back to the United States. A complete V-2 was examined and found to be somewhat like Robert Goddard's rockets, only far more advanced. With the war with Japan still raging, the United States wanted to jump-start its nascent rocket program, and the easiest way to do that was to adopt German V-2 engineers, parts, components, and systems.

On June 20, 1945, von Braun and the other members of his rocket team were assigned to America as part of a mission known as Operation Overcast. At first, von Braun worried that they would be questioned and then sent back to stand trial for war crimes, but their advanced knowledge about ballistic missiles was too valuable to waste. Under Operation Overcast and then Operation Paperclip, the U.S. government made sure not to prosecute the Nazi scientists for war crimes. They were issued security clearances to work on U.S. Army projects and assigned to Fort Bliss near El Paso, Texas. They were told to start rocketry work on the nearby White Sands Missile Range in New Mexico.

From a military perspective, Operation Paperclip was a great success. Von Braun taught American rocket experts how the V-2 worked, then he showed the Americans how to build the missiles from leftover parts that had been recovered. He shared everything he knew with his new U.S. Army colleagues, despite the fact that not long before he'd been designing intercontinental missiles to obliterate London and perhaps even New York City someday. Now he was helping the U.S. Army build up their own ballistic missile capabilities, while continuing to hope his research might someday lead to a moon rocket.

chapter six

A New Enemy

In the entire twentieth century, splitting the atom during World War II was the only technological feat equal in achievement to the American moonshot. The birth of the Nuclear Age took place with the Trinity test in Alamogordo, New Mexico, on July 16, 1945. Then, on August 6, the bomber Enola Gay dropped the first atomic bomb, nicknamed "Little Boy," on Hiroshima, Japan. Within four months, the acute effects of the bombing killed 90,000 to 146,000 people. On August 9, a second atomic bomb, "Fat Man," was dropped on the city of Nagasaki, killing at least 70,000 more people instantly. Most of both cities were turned into irradiated wastelands. After the catastrophic attacks, the Japanese surrendered on August 14, 1945, which became known as V-J Day, or "Victory over Japan" day.

The atomic bomb ushered in an age in which human beings held the godlike power to end life on Earth. During the war, Germany's V-2 program had been pushed along by fears that the United States was developing a similar rocket of its own—which it hadn't been. At the same time, America's atomic bomb program was developed for fear that Germany was also working on an atomic bomb—which it hadn't really been. In fact, the United States and Germany were focused on different technological strategies. That meant that at the end of World War II, the United States held a virtual monopoly on both advanced rocketry and atomic weapon technologies.

According to the federal government, at the close of the war, the United States had been eight years behind the Germans in rocket capability. With von Braun and the German scientists now on American soil, that gap vanished overnight. With the postwar world quickly realigning into an ideological struggle between the Western democracies and Soviet communism, the Soviets saw this development as a clear threat, and Stalin decided that closing the ballistic missile gap would be a top secret national priority.

In El Paso, von Braun and his rocket team worked on developing rockets and ballistic missiles capable of launching satellites into space. The German immigrants were considered wards of the Army. They had no passports or visas, their mail was censored, and they weren't allowed off the Army base without an escort. They weren't prisoners, but they couldn't move to other parts of the United States. Von Braun called himself a

POP—"prisoner of peace"—rather than a POW, or prisoner of war. Despite these constraints, the engineers were well paid; von Braun himself earned $6,000 a year, more than twice the average American income at the time.

Although isolated, the German engineers knew they were lucky to have escaped what could have been much worse fates after the war. Rocket scientists in Russian-occupied East Germany faced the threat of being kidnapped and forced to live and work under house arrest in the Soviet Union. Ultimately, the Soviets employed four thousand German rocketeers, and operated several V-2 assembly lines.

In the United States, the engineers continued to make steady progress on their rocket design. The first V-2 launch in the United States occurred over the New Mexico desert in the spring of 1946, with the test rocket soaring to an altitude of sixty-seven miles. Over the next five years, about seventy tests were conducted of V-2s and related rockets, and two-thirds of them were successful.

Although von Braun dreamed of traveling to the moon, it could not be denied that his rockets were ideally suited to be used as weapons. The U.S. government was intensely interested in making ballistic missile investments, but at the time there was limited interest in funding rocketry for peaceful purposes, such as manned space exploration and satellite telecommunications. When a deputy commander of the Army Air Force tried to convince the war department to support the launch of an unmanned V-2 to explore space for peace, his request was denied.

• • •

In the spring of 1945, as von Braun was busy negotiating his surrender to the Americans, Jack Kennedy was in San Francisco reporting for Hearst newspapers about a charter for the new United Nations, an organization being developed to encourage world peace and cooperation. When he completed the assignment, his father arranged for him to tour Germany and visit other European capitals.

After witnessing the devastation on both sides of the war (Europe and the Pacific), Jack returned to the States, where his father had begun to orchestrate his political career. With his older brother gone, Jack became the vehicle of his father's political ambition. Joseph Sr. worked with a lecture bureau to line up speaking engagements for Jack. He hired political advisors to organize a congressional campaign in Massachusetts's eleventh district. Fulfilling his father's wishes, in early 1946 Jack announced his run for the seat.

Although he was smart, handsome, and a war hero, he didn't have much in common with the working-class voters in his district's factory cities. He was also young and didn't belong to any of the local clubs. Some protestants in Massachusetts were biased against him because he was Roman Catholic. But Jack was a sincere candidate who spent long days meeting voters throughout the district. He knew that people worried about the economy. Many voters considered President Harry Truman an ineffective leader, and the Democratic Party was struggling to define itself after Franklin D. Roosevelt's four-term presidency.

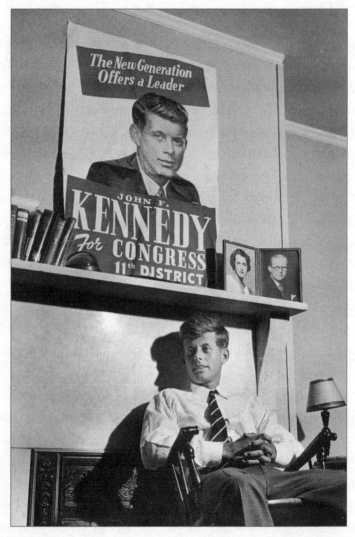

Congressional candidate John F. Kennedy leans back in a chair under a shelf that holds up a 1946 campaign poster ("The New Generation Offers a Leader") and photos of his parents, Joseph and Rose, in his office-room at the Bellevue Hotel, Boston, Massachusetts.

Tensions between the United States and the Soviet Union were increasing. Distrust between the two countries intensified as the Cold War hostilities escalated, stopping just short of open warfare. Many considered Stalin the new Hitler, a dictator bent on creating a communist world order. The United States and Western allies felt they needed to unite against the tide of communist expansion. At home, people began to worry that communists were working behind the scenes at every level of American society. Many people were easily led by their fears, leading to a "red scare" in which innocent people were wrongly accused of subversion.

Jack was already an outspoken critic of communism, and anti-communism became a strong part of his platform. His experiences overseas had given him a firsthand look at the world, and he was comfortable criticizing everything from Soviet concentration camps in Siberia to the Kremlin's repression of journalists. Kennedy favored a tough new liberalism that would extend civil rights while standing up to fascists and communists. At the same time, he held on to his bright-eyed idealism about America being a proud nation of immigrants. Idealistic at heart, he pushed for peace in every discussion of foreign affairs.

Kennedy was one of the youngest candidates running for federal office in 1946, but he embraced the spirit of his time. "The war made us get serious for the first time in our lives," Kennedy said. "We've been serious ever since, and we show no signs of stopping." He also knew the dawn of the Atomic Age had focused that seriousness in a way nothing before it ever had. "What we do now will shape the history of civilization for many years to come," he said in his first major speech. "We have a weary world trying to bind up the wounds of a fierce struggle. That is dire enough. What is infinitely far worse is that we have a world which has unleashed the terrible powers of atomic energy. We have a world capable of destroying itself."

On November 5, 1946, at age twenty-nine, Jack Kennedy was elected a U.S. representative for the Eleventh Congressional District in Boston.

At the same time Kennedy was beginning his political career, von Braun was becoming more outspoken about space travel. In the fall of 1946, the scientist made his first public speech in America, to the El Paso Rotary Club. "It seems to be a law of nature that all novel technical inventions that have a future for civilian use start out as weapons," he said. He went on to predict a future in which rocketry took its proper role of propelling satellites and space stations into orbit and powering missions to the moon and beyond. This was his dream for the future. His remarks earned cheers and thunderous applause.

Once again, von Braun's ideas were ahead of their time. Before his space dreams could take flight, rocketry would enter new and even more dangerous territory with the military's development of the first intercontinental ballistic missiles, and their ultimate pairing with atomic warheads. This was the threatening reality in which he was destined to play an outsized role, and it was the world in which Jack Kennedy was beginning his public career. While von Braun's imagination soared to the moon and beyond, at this phase of his life all he could do was work on military rockets for the U.S. Army. Kennedy, for his part, was both an idealist and an ardent anticommunist, favoring the creation of an international body to oversee atomic weapons while knowing such a body would also help maintain America's monopoly on the technology.

Part II
GENERATION SPUTNIK

chapter seven

And Then There Were Two

In the postwar years, the United States was spending vast amounts of money on financial assistance to nations devastated during World War II. Secretary of State George C. Marshall designed a plan that pumped more than $13 billion ($140 billion in today's dollars) into rebuilding Western Europe. The money was intended to stabilize currencies, promote industrial and agricultural production, and strengthen international trade. A similar rebuilding program was offered in Japan.

Many parts of the Soviet Union had also been flattened by the war, so most Americans assumed that the Kremlin would focus its postwar efforts on rebuilding the country's infrastructure. Instead, they were secretly devoting enormous resources to developing nuclear weapons and rockets of their own. By 1946, with the support of the German scientists they'd captured at the end of the war, the Soviet rocketry program was working on ballistic missiles with a range of nearly 2,000 miles. Meanwhile, Soviet scientists also worked on developing an atomic bomb, procuring uranium ore mined in the Belgian Congo.

While the Soviets raced ahead in secret, the U.S. military squabbled. With budgets down from their wartime levels, the various branches of the armed services fought for funding. Rocket development continued on various tracks across the armed forces, without a coordinated program.

In an attempt to focus their efforts, Major General Curtis LeMay, a war hero then serving as the Air Force's deputy chief of air staff for research and development, commissioned an outside contractor to prepare a report answering two questions: How could satellites benefit the U.S. military? and How could space travel advance humanity? The contractor's response was a 321-page report describing future military uses for satellites, including surveillance and missile guidance, as well as civilian uses in communication and meteorology. It concluded that a satellite vehicle with appropriate instrumentation would become one of the most revolutionary military, scientific, and communication tools of the twentieth century. At a top secret meeting, military officials discussed combining forces to work on a joint satellite project, but the parties couldn't agree on a plan.

Instead, different branches of the military designed their own rocket and missile programs. The Navy moved forward in 1946 with the development of the Viking rocket, which was designed to gather atmospheric data to predict the weather. It borrowed from the V-2, but it was a distinctly American effort. Test launches of the Viking carried research instruments to altitudes of up to 158 miles.

A captured German V-2 rocket just after takeoff at Launching Complex 33 at White Sands Missile Range in New Mexico. The launch was part of an experimental program carried out by the U.S. Army's Upper Atmosphere Research Panel.

The Army continued with its own missile project, relying heavily on German technology and expertise. In the fall of 1948, it began to develop Earth-orbiting satellites. The Pentagon had been convinced of the satellite's potential not only for surveillance and communications but also for intimidation, suggesting that the "mere presence in the sky of an artificial satellite would have a strong psychological effect on the potential enemy."

In addition to studying how to explore space, Americans were also making aviation history within the Earth's atmosphere. On October 14, 1947, test pilot Chuck Yeager flew the Bell X-1 experimental aircraft to an altitude of 43,000 feet and a speed of 700 miles per hour, becoming the first person to travel faster than the speed of sound. Yeager should have become an instant hero, but his mission was kept top secret by the Air Force for years.

In postwar America, the military weren't the only ones taking to the skies. With a surplus of skilled pilots trained for the war, commercial aviation took off as airlines began to establish fixed routes across the country. Wartime technologies also aided this move to the skies, including electronic navigation and anti-icing technology that allowed for all-weather flying. Every year, more and more Americans were using commercial aviation as a means of long-distance travel.

Congressman Jack Kennedy proved to be a successful representative from his district, and he was reelected to a second term in 1948. He earned a reputation for excellent constituent service, and he was well liked on Capitol Hill. He usually voted with fellow Democrats, but he thought for himself and voted his conscience. However, critics carped that he was more of a show horse than workhorse on Capitol Hill.

While in Congress, Kennedy continued exercising his interest in global affairs. He supported the United States when it joined Belgium, Canada, Denmark, France, Ireland, Italy, Luxembourg, the Netherlands, Norway, Portugal, and the United Kingdom in creating the North Atlantic Treaty Organization (NATO) on April 4, 1949. NATO's primary goal was to resist Soviet expansion. This Atlantic alliance of democratic nations still exists today.

Kennedy also followed the issues surrounding nuclear weapons. At the time, the United States was the only country to have an atomic bomb, but Soviet leader Joseph Stalin was determined to catch up. American intelligence continued to underestimate the Soviets and believed them incapable of developing atomic capabilities. However, all that changed on September 22, 1949, when the United States learned that the Soviet Union had in fact detonated its first atomic bomb, nicknamed Joe 1, three weeks earlier. Global affairs were about to get much more dangerous and complicated.

The world order had changed. There were now two nuclear superpowers. President Harry Truman not only worried about nuclear attack from the Soviet Union but also that his administration would be blamed for allowing the Soviets to develop the technology in the first place.

When Congressman Kennedy heard about the Soviet threat, he initially focused on the need for improved civil defense. He felt the country needed to plan ways to resist or respond to an atomic attack. Kennedy endorsed the idea of government-printed pamphlets warning about post-explosion radiation hazards, and advocated having schoolchildren learn to seek shelter in case of an attack. But his approach was too simple.

On the other side of the Capitol, Connecticut senator Brien McMahon had earned a reputation in Congress as an expert on atomic technology. As chair of the Senate Special Committee on Atomic Energy, McMahon became known as "Mr. Atomic Bomb" because he wrote the Atomic Energy Act of 1946, which sought to control nuclear weapons development and nuclear power management, stripping this authority from the military.

Senator McMahon knew that preventing World War III would be more complicated than passing out civil defense pamphlets. It would take both diplomacy and the willpower to build a nuclear arsenal that could outpace the Soviets. If Russia could blow up America fifteen times over, the U.S. had to build enough weapons to wipe out the Soviet Union fifty times. That was the type of hawkish thinking that had taken hold in Washington. McMahon's more-is-better thinking became central to the battle for nuclear supremacy, framing the Cold War until the collapse of the Soviet Union in 1991.

Kennedy argued for a more conventional approach, saying that the best way to avoid atomic war was for the United States to increase its troop levels. He favored spending billions on modernizing the military and remaining a permanent state of wartime readiness. Both Kennedy and McMahon blamed President Harry Truman, in part, for Stalin's advancements.

Just a month after news of the Soviet atom bomb broke, the world order suffered a second blow when the Chinese Nationalist government fell to the communists in October 1949. It was a double whammy that sent many Americans into a panic. They feared that communism would spread across the globe, ultimately destroying capitalism and the American way of life.

chapter eight

Into the Space Race

The combination of the Soviet atom bomb and the Communist Chinese revolution strengthened Congressman John F. Kennedy's anti-communist position. In April 1950, while Kennedy was approaching his third congressional race, President Truman received a top secret report that urged a massive buildup of America's military forces and nuclear arsenal to counter the Soviet threat. This hunger for more and better weapons justified the space race and laid the groundwork for Cold War policy for the next two decades.

The new approach was almost immediately put to the test. On June 25, 1950, the Soviet-backed North Korean Army invaded South Korea. Fearing the invasion could be a prelude to wider communist aggression across Asia, the Truman administration quickly ordered U.S. forces to aid South Korea.

In the United Nations Security Council, the United States rushed through a resolution denouncing the North Koreans as aggressors and demanding the withdrawal of their troops. This was the first time the United Nations had given permission to a member state to halt and punish aggression.

U.S. forces began arriving in Korea in July. Although twenty-one countries contributed troops to the UN multinational force, 90 percent of the soldiers were American. Kennedy fully supported the armed forces and called for enormous increases in military spending. He criticized President Truman's foreign policy as not being even tougher on the Soviets. Kennedy was a traditional liberal on domestic issues—he supported Social Security, the minimum wage, education, and using tax revenues to address societal needs—but he was also an anti-Soviet, pro-military hawk. He won reelection for Congress in November 1950.

In 1951, Kennedy strengthened his anti-Soviet position by spending five weeks in Europe and then testifying before the Senate Foreign Relations and Armed Services committees on how to defend Europe against Soviet control. Rumors began to swirl that he would run for Senate the following year.

When not focused on his political career, Kennedy enjoyed his personal life, which gossip columnists liked to cover. He enjoyed parties and going out on the town. In May 1951, he met Jacqueline Bouvier at a dinner party and he was attracted to her, but he wasn't yet ready for marriage. Some people who knew him well thought he was living recklessly, as though death was knocking. At age thirty-four, he was already five years older than his brother Joe had been when he died in the war. That death haunted him, as did the death of his younger sister Kathleen, who'd perished in a plane crash three years before, at age twenty-eight. Jack himself was, in fact, in poor health. In addition to the digestive and neurological problems he'd suffered since childhood, he also had back problems, causing periods of blinding pain that forced him to sometimes rely on crutches. In 1947 he had been diagnosed with Addison's disease, a problem with the adrenal gland that causes fatigue, abdominal and muscle pain, and depression, among other symptoms.

His health challenges and personal losses may have contributed to Kennedy's urgency in life. Though still a young man, Jack may have felt he was living on borrowed time, and he wanted to accomplish his personal and political goals as soon as possible.

In 1950, Wernher von Braun and about two hundred German scientists and engineers working in the United States were relocated from El Paso to Huntsville, Alabama, to work on what became the U.S. Army's Redstone ballistic missiles. In Huntsville the von Braun team engineered ballistic missiles called Redstone, Jupiter-C, Juno, and the Saturn 1B. Like Kennedy, von Braun was eager to make his mark; he wanted to build rockets and make history. Fearing that the Soviet Union was beating the United States in the design and manufacture of missiles, he complained to his superiors that the

U.S. government was developing rockets "at a tempo for peace."

Dr. Wernher von Braun (right) with President Dwight D. Eisenhower (center) at dedication of Marshall Space Flight Center (Huntsville, Alabama). Eisenhower never fully trusted von Braun because of his Nazi past.

Beginning with von Braun's new Redstone ballistic missiles (which were direct descendants of his V-2 rockets), Huntsville became a crucial center of Cold War ballistic missile technology. Faced with fighting a North Korean military that received equipment from the Soviet Union and China, it was essential that the United States step up its missile production for military purposes before working on manned space voyages.

Although he was only thirty-four years old, Kennedy ran for Senate in 1952, taking on popular Republican senator Henry Cabot Lodge Jr. Kennedy could have waited two years to face a more vulnerable opponent for Massachusetts's other Senate seat, but he didn't want to waste the time. A seasoned politician, the fifty-year-old Lodge was a moderate Republican from a prominent family. During World War II, he had resigned from the Senate to serve in the military, then returned to win another election that brought him back to the Senate.

Kennedy waged a serious fight. He traveled tirelessly, appearing before hundreds of small groups. Taken together, these small events added up to hundreds of thousands of voters. Kennedy also benefited from Lodge's political mistakes. The senator made the strategic error of backing moderate Dwight Eisenhower (who had been supreme allied commander of the war's D-Day invasion) over conservative Robert Taft Jr. for the Republican presidential nomination. This angered the right wing of his party, which stayed home on Election Day.

To the surprise of many, Kennedy won. Republican presidential candidate Eisenhower also won, becoming the first Republican to occupy the White House in twenty years.

In his new role in the Senate, Kennedy tried to avoid rookie mistakes. He pushed for projects that helped the country more broadly, not just his Massachusetts voters. As a senator, eloquence and manners were expected, and Kennedy fit right in, with the education and erudition to quote poetry and cite Roman philosophers when he spoke. Senator Kennedy valued the power of his new seat. He felt that many congressmen had little real authority, but he realized that every senator had real clout. Congressmen serve two-year terms and are constantly preparing for reelection, while senators are elected for six-year terms.

Kennedy knew he needed a signature issue to define him in the Senate, and he thought he saw it in the new president's military policies. To Kennedy's surprise, he realized he was actually more hawkishly militaristic than Eisenhower, the hero of the largest armed offensive in history. Eisenhower did not want to unnecessarily grow the military. Only five months after taking office, he pulled America out of the Korean War, which had cost more than 34,000 U.S. lives. He then ordered a considerable reduction in military spending, and questioned the stability of an economy dependent on weapons production for economic prosperity. When he left office eight years later, Eisenhower famously warned about the dangers of "the military-industrial complex." Injecting his voice into the national debate, Kennedy complained that the president's "New Look" defense strategy lacked coherence.

• • •

Although Eisenhower favored a smaller military than Truman during the Korean War, he did support air power. The Air Force had not prioritized the development of intercontinental ballistic missiles at a level comparable to the Soviets, and he realized that America needed to catch up.

Von Braun was more than ready to do his part to help the U.S. have more sophisticated missiles than the Soviets. He test-fired his Redstone missile at Cape Canaveral, Florida, beginning the rocket's career as the workhorse of the Army's missile program, used as the launch vehicle for a number of different missions. From 1952–1954, hoping to engage the public in space travel, von Braun published a series of articles in *Collier's* magazine, a popular periodical that reached four million readers. He argued that traveling to the moon and Mars would be doable in his lifetime. He warned that the United States must "immediately embark on a long-range missile development program" or lose out to the Soviet Union. A master at media spin, he realized that in a democracy where taxpayers paid the bills, his dreams of space exploration would only become real if the American public supported them, and that would only happen through a campaign to beat Russia in ballistic missiles, develop new space technology, and eventually gain the international prestige of being first in manned space exploration.

On September 2, 1953, Jack Kennedy married Jacqueline Bouvier at an elaborate wedding in Newport, Rhode Island. "Jackie" had grown up in a wealthy family which had homes in

Manhattan; East Hampton, Long Island; McLean, Virginia; and Newport, Rhode Island. She spoke fluent French and loved horses.

While the Kennedys were on their honeymoon, a report commissioned by the Truman administration nineteen months earlier was delivered to Eisenhower, titled "The Present Status of the Satellite Problem." This report laid out the propaganda benefits that would go to the Soviets if they were able to launch a satellite before the United States. The report recommended that the government set up a committee of top engineers and scientists to determine what steps should be taken to launch a U.S. satellite into outer space.

Allen Dulles, the director of the Central Intelligence Agency (CIA), also understood that the United States needed to lead the world in satellite technology, which had the potential to revolutionize telecommunications, weather prediction, navigation, and surveillance. He warned that if the Soviets beat the United States in satellites, it would be a major Cold War setback. "There is little doubt but what the nation that first successfully launches the Earth satellite, and thereby introduces the age of space travel, will gain incalculable international prestige and recognition," Dulles said. "Our scientific community as well as the nation would gain invaluable respect and confidence should our country be the first to launch the satellite."

In the summer of 1954, Kennedy was in poor health. He was suffering chronic pain due to college football and war injuries, as well as osteoporosis caused by steroid treatments for his colitis and failing adrenal glands. He also underwent dangerous back surgery, for which he was given only a 50-50 chance of surviving. Because of his age and appearance, however, most people still saw him as young and vigorous. In fact, when Senate Majority Leader Lyndon Johnson suffered a heart attack in 1955, Kennedy's stature in the Senate rose because his colleagues saw him as healthy and vital compared to the ailing Johnson.

There was talk that Kennedy might get the vice-presidential spot on the Democrats' 1956 presidential ticket. While the chance of beating Eisenhower was a long shot, several powerful Democrats, including Lyndon Johnson, wanted to run for the top spot. At the Democratic National Convention, Illinois governor Adlai Stevenson was ultimately chosen as the Democratic presidential candidate, and Kennedy was among those who wanted to join the ticket as vice president. Though he assumed Stevenson would lose to the popular Eisenhower, Kennedy figured the vice-presidential slot would give him national attention and put him in position for the top of the ticket in 1960, when Eisenhower would have completed his second and last term. Ultimately, Senator Estes Kefauver of Tennessee won the spot, but the experience proved that Kennedy could be taken seriously at the presidential level.

After the Democratic ticket of Stevenson-Kefauver lost that November, Kennedy began preparing his run for the White House in 1960.

• • •

In early 1957, Senator Kennedy began publicly criticizing President Eisenhower for allowing the United States to lag behind the Soviet Union in the number of nuclear missiles and bombs in its arsenal. Although Eisenhower had designated the Air Force's Atlas missile program a top national priority in 1954, Kennedy didn't think that went far enough. Kennedy's argument caught fire on August 26, 1957, when the Soviets announced that they'd successfully tested the first nuclear-tipped intercontinental ballistic missile capable of reaching the United States.

Kennedy railed against Eisenhower policies that, he claimed, had led to Soviet domination in missile development. Having been raised in a family obsessed with winning, Kennedy reduced Cold War statesmanship to a contest. Who was first? Who was ahead? Who had more?

When at long last the U.S. Air Force launched its first Atlas rocket on June 11, 1957, it blew up twenty-four seconds after taking off. Kennedy used Eisenhower's apparent indifference to technology as a political issue by focusing on the "missile gap" between the United States and the Soviet Union. Experts questioned the relevance of numerical advantage when it came to missiles, given that so many other factors had an impact on a weapon's potency. They also wondered where Kennedy got his data that the United States was lagging. By any measure, the "gap" was far closer than Kennedy let on.

But Kennedy was right that the Soviets had turned

rocketry into a potent military weapon. As long as Soviet leader Joseph Stalin was alive, the Soviet Union acted as though World War II had never ended. From 1945 until his death in 1953, Stalin gave priority to the development of atomic weapons and intercontinental ballistic missiles that would give his nation the strength to deter its enemies. Stalin's single-minded focus on military technology weakened the Soviet economy by neglecting the development of consumer goods and other civilian needs.

Eisenhower wanted to avoid a missile competition with the Soviet Union, worried the effort would ultimately lead to nuclear war. He would have preferred to use the money spent on rockets to improve America's highways, seaways, and schools.

However, he did recognize the value of developing space technologies for peaceful purposes, and in 1955 took concrete steps in that direction. Three years before, the International Council of Scientific Unions had proposed that an International Geophysical Year be celebrated during a high point of sunspot activity between July 1957 and December 1958. The idea was that scientists from sixty-seven countries and four thousand research institutions would coordinate their research on the Earth and its physical properties and processes, and share their data. Promoted by the United Nations, the effort had the support of both the United States and the Soviet Union, and both superpowers announced plans to launch research satellites in the name of global peace.

Eisenhower didn't want to rush a satellite launch just to

prove U.S. superiority. Instead, he decided to greenlight development of a project based on the Navy's Viking rocket. Both the Army and Air Force had rocket programs already in place that could have launched a satellite into space in the summer of 1957 if they'd received adequate funding, but Eisenhower preferred the Viking because it had been designed for peaceful meteorological research.

Von Braun was livid at the president's decision. "It is a contest to get a satellite into orbit, and we [the Army] are way ahead on this," he said. Von Braun had to accept the president's decision. All he could do was wait for another president who might favor fast-tracking Army satellites and even more ambitious space voyages.

chapter nine

Sputnik Revolution

Jack Kennedy met Wernher von Braun for the first time in New York City in 1953. They were at an event for *Time* magazine and had an hour to talk and get to know each other. The two bonded over shared memories of World War II, Kennedy discussing the details of how his older brother had died in an aviation accident. "I remember that he said the accident occurred with an obsolescent type of bomb aircraft that had been loaded to the gills with explosives," von Braun said in 1964.

It was a strange kind of bonding. Kennedy's brother had died trying to stop the very rockets von Braun was designing and building for Hitler. Now, though, their shared enemy was the Soviet Union, and they were both working to achieve United States supremacy in missile and satellite technology.

President John F. Kennedy (center) with Vice President Lyndon Johnson (right)
listening intently to Dr. Wernher von Braun (left) explain the models of the Saturn
C-1 booster rocket during their inspection tour of the Space Flight Center.

Kennedy was pleased that von Braun and his former Nazi rocket team were now leading the effort for Team America. "He had been following the work of myself and my associates in missile development with the greatest interest," von Braun said.

World leaders like American president Dwight Eisenhower and the Soviet Union's new premier, Nikita Khrushchev (who eventually ascended to the role after Stalin's death that March), had been born in the nineteenth century. Kennedy and von Braun were twentieth-century futurists who understood that time was divided into pre V-2 versus post V-2, pre Hiroshima versus post Hiroshima. These powerful weapons of mass destruction had changed the balance of global power. Armies and naval forces could now be wiped out with long-range nuclear missiles. Both Kennedy and von Braun feared that technological progress in America was coming too slowly, and that the Kremlin had already gained the upper hand over the United States in space technology. This fear seemingly became reality on the night of October 4, 1957, when radio operators working at the Naval Research Laboratory in Washington, D.C., picked up a steady A-flat beep from an onboard transmitter. They identified the sound as a signal from a Soviet satellite in Earth's orbit.

The device, named Sputnik—"traveling companion of the world" in Russian—had been launched into orbit aboard a modified intercontinental ballistic missile. It carried equipment to analyze the density and temperature of the upper atmosphere. Amateur astronomers also picked up the signal and a few of them ran outside and saw the strange object streaking across the skies.

The next morning, the naval laboratory announced that a Soviet satellite had successfully orbited the Earth. Khrushchev confirmed the report, adding that the weight of this "artificial moon" was 184 pounds, and its shape was a ball about twenty-two inches in diameter, with four antennas sticking out of it. The satellite orbited the Earth elliptically every ninety minutes at an altitude of 140 to 560 miles. Sputnik was similar to technology on the planning boards of the U.S. Armed Forces. Nevertheless, the Soviets had achieved their feat first.

Sputnik stunned millions of Americans, shattering the public assumption that the United States held technological advantage over the Soviet Union. The world was captivated by the polished sphere of aluminum, magnesium, and titanium that had pushed beyond the bounds of Earth, extending the hand of man and changing ideas of what was possible.

Without the tension of the Cold War, the Soviet launch might have been celebrated as a scientific accomplishment equal to Marie Curie's discovery of radium or Guglielmo Marconi's invention of the radio. But with so little trust between the two superpowers, many Americans took the Sputnik news like a punch in the nose rather than a shared human accomplishment. If the Soviets could launch a satellite into space, they reasoned, then maybe they could also destroy parts of the United States with nuclear-armed missiles.

Democrats stirred up paranoia for political gain. Many

politicians unfairly charged President Eisenhower for being asleep at the wheel. For his part, Kennedy deemed Sputnik a national humiliation and insisted that America needed far stronger ballistic missile and satellite programs if it wanted to beat the Soviets. Senate Majority Leader Lyndon Johnson became the most high-profile Democratic critic. "The Roman Empire controlled the world because it could build roads," he said. "Later—when men moved to the sea—the British Empire was dominant because it had ships. In the Air Age, we were powerful because we had airplanes. Now the Communists have established a foothold in outer space." It seemed as if America was tied down to lonely Planet Earth while the Soviet Union was soaring through outer space, reaching for the stars. Johnson's alarmist reaction resounded on Capitol Hill, and is frequently cited by Cold War scholars as the tipping point in the push to create a unified American space program.

Despite the criticism, President Eisenhower took the launch in stride. He noted that space had been around a long time, and it wasn't going anywhere. To Eisenhower, it didn't matter who happened to be first to circle the Earth with an artificial moon. He insisted that democracy's superiority over communism didn't need hype or promotion; it spoke for itself.

Eisenhower also knew that the U.S. satellite program in late 1957 was essentially equal to or even more advanced than the Soviet program, but what mattered during the Cold War was public perception. In the Senate, Johnson called for an official investigation to gauge the reasons behind America's apparently weak satellite program. He used these hearings to increase his stature as he eyed the 1960 Democratic nomination for president.

Kennedy, also looking toward the 1960 election, made his first formal remarks about "the age of Sputnik" on October 18, 1957. He mocked Eisenhower's indifference and argued that surpassing the Soviets in satellite technology would require the U.S. government to fund a civilian space agency. He argued that the U.S. public education system was inferior to that of the Soviet Union, and that schools needed to better prepare children in fields of the future, such as engineering, physics, and mathematics. He warned that the U.S. was "losing the satellite and missile race because of complacent miscalculations, penny-pinching, budget cutbacks, incredibly confused management, and wasteful rivalries and jealousies."

For the several hundred dedicated scientists and engineers working in U.S. space rocketry programs, the Sputnik launch was troubling. Von Braun took the news hard. When a reporter told him about Sputnik, he winced, stung by the news. He had been disappointed that Eisenhower hadn't supported greater funding for space research, and now he hoped Sputnik would force the president to change his position. While the Soviets claimed their space program was for peaceful scientific purposes, American intelligence indicated that its funding came from the Ministry of Defense, and the project's mastermind had also designed the first transcontinental ballistic missile.

Less than a month after the first Sputnik success, the

Soviets launched Sputnik 2 on November 3, 1957. This time, the satellite carried the first living creature ever to orbit the Earth: Laika, a dark-beige mixed-breed dog. With a dog on board, the media began calling Sputnik 2 "Muttnik" or "Pooch-nik." Laika became the mascot of the Soviet Union, appearing on commemorative buttons, plates, and other souvenirs.

The Soviets had the technology to send a dog into space, but they hadn't solved one essential problem: how to get the dog safely back to Earth. Laika died in space from dehydration, overheating, and stress. Sputnik 2 proved that a living creature could survive for hours in a weightless environment, but by failing to protect the dog, the Soviets opened themselves up to accusations of brutality and disregard for life—and made U.S. policy makers suspect that the Soviets were skipping steps in their research in an effort to be first in space.

Soviet Premier Khrushchev considered Laika's short trip into space another victory over the United States. In January 1958, *Time* magazine named Khrushchev "Man of the Year" for 1957, and the cover illustration showed him holding the Sputnik satellite in his hands. In the article, the Soviet leader bragged that his country had "outstripped the leading capitalist country—the United States—in the field of scientific and technical progress."

While Khrushchev took the limelight, Eisenhower remained unrattled by all the Space Age hullabaloo. To Kennedy, this made the president seem out of step with the future.

Sputnik 2 amplified the criticism of America's space

program. Nuclear weapons designer Edward Teller said the U.S. had lost "a battle more important and great than Pearl Harbor." Kennedy doubled down in his criticism of Eisenhower. Earlier in his career, Kennedy gave no hard answers to questions about space supremacy, waiting for other politicians to weigh in before he took a stand. But now Kennedy had matured into a leader ready to speak out clearly and aggressively.

Scheduled to address a group in Topeka, Kansas, five days after the launch of Sputnik 2, Kennedy addressed the issue of "Science and Security." In his remarks, he slammed the president in his home state, complaining of weak leadership on space technology and science education. He named the areas in which he thought Eisenhower had failed, including insufficient funding for satellites, a lack of cooperation and coordination among military services and private contractors, and duplication of efforts in research and development. "It is now apparent that we could have been first with the satellite," Kennedy said, "but failed to see any reason for doing so, failed to see the scientific, military, and propaganda advantage it would give to the Soviets if they were first."

The press applauded Kennedy's remarks. He also got a boost from *Life* magazine, which printed a long feature comparing American and Soviet students at the high school level. The article focused on a Moscow school where the students studied physics and algebra six days a week, comparing it with a Chicago school where students goofed off and didn't take challenging classes. Kennedy responded by supporting the National

Defense Education Act, which increased funding for what are now known as STEM subjects in schools: science, technology, engineering, and math. It also created the first federal student loan program to encourage students to participate in higher education.

Soon after the launch of Sputnik 2, Soviet Minister of Defense Nikolai Bulganin was asked by the *New York Times* when his country would launch a third satellite. "It's the Americans' turn now," he said.

Von Braun was ruffled by the comments. He and his Huntsville missile men were frustrated and confused about why the government didn't pay more attention to the emerging technology. They had been ordered to concentrate on missile development and set aside work on satellites and space exploration.

While the nation was focused on Sputnik, President Eisenhower had been distracted by other issues demanding his attention. Eisenhower had been at his farm in Gettysburg, Pennsylvania, when he learned about the Sputnik launch. He had spent all day in meetings involving the situation in Little Rock, Arkansas, where segregationists supported by the state's governor were preventing nine African American students from integrating an all-white high school. Instead of coming up with a thoughtful statement to the country regarding Sputnik, Eisenhower asked the White House press secretary to explain his feeling that the Soviet accomplishment "did not come as a surprise" and that the U.S. wasn't "in a race" with the Kremlin.

Eisenhower credited the Soviet success to "all the German scientists" who had been captured at the end of World War II and taken to Moscow. This comment further embarrassed von Braun, who knew the best and brightest German scientists were actually in the United States. He knew that the difference in success had to do with the resources they had to work with, not the skills of the rocket engineers.

Von Braun urged the government to support the Army's satellite program with funds reflecting the urgency the historical moment demanded. "For God's sake turn us loose and let us do something," von Braun said. "We can put up the satellite in sixty days." Von Braun's commander gave him ninety days to get the job done. Moving quickly, von Braun reserved a late January launch date and began frantic preparations.

chapter ten

Keeping Up with the Kremlin

The Soviet Union's successes with Sputnik, particularly the global media windfall the Kremlin reaped, caught the United States somewhat off guard. Suddenly, launching an American satellite became an urgent concern. After initially dismissing the achievement, the White House changed its position and announced that the United States would send "small satellite spheres" into orbit by late in the year.

Wernher von Braun and his Army team were left scrambling. They had been planning to launch test vehicles by the end of the year, with an actual satellite launch planned for the following spring, powered by a Redstone rocket. Now they had to finish the task by December.

Parallel to the Army's Redstone program, the U.S. Navy also accelerated its own Vanguard rocket program. On Friday,

December 6, 1957, Vanguard engineers, technicians, and high-ranking officials gathered at Cape Canaveral, Florida, for the first Vanguard launch. Located on scrubland and sandy beach facing the Atlantic Ocean, Cape Canaveral had been used by the military since 1949 because of its ideal geography. It was on the East Coast, so it offered an aerial boost from the Earth's spin. Being closer to the equator also made it marginally easier to achieve orbit. And it was far away from heavily populated areas: If there was a rocket accident, the ocean could absorb the crash, with no debris falling on civilians.

The military had already completed some rocket tests at Cape Canaveral by the time the three-stage Vanguard TV3 rocket was ready. The rocket stood seventy-two feet in height, and it would be propelled by two liquid-fueled sections or "stages." The third stage, carrying a small satellite, would be propelled to its final orbital trajectory by a solid-fuel motor. The sections had to be kept separate and timed meticulously.

Reporters crowded Cape Canaveral for the landmark Vanguard TV3 launch, which was covered on live television. Millions watched as the rocket took off, rose four feet into the air . . . then dropped back to Earth and exploded in a fireball. The battered satellite was thrown to the side when the rocket hit the ground, rolling around on the launchpad in a cloud of black soot.

Although they were embarrassed by the unimpressive outcome, scientists consider a test a success if something new is learned. Researchers learned a lot from the failure of the TV3, but the public considered it a massive failure, and commentators quickly dubbed it "Kaputnik," "Stayputnik," and "Flopnik." Fortunately, the engineers had a spare rocket—named TV3BU for "Back Up"—but they wanted to improve it before they repeated the experiment. The rocket engineers knew this second rocket would have to be ready to go within a couple of months, and it had to be successful.

Senator Kennedy didn't comment on Flopnik. He was dealing with a public relations problem of his own. The day after the launch, a journalist alleged that Kennedy had not been the real author of *Profiles in Courage*, a book for which he'd won a Pulitzer Prize in 1957. According to the reporter, the book had actually been written by Kennedy speechwriter Ted Sorensen. This was a strike against Kennedy's image as someone who played aboveboard. Kennedy's family fought the accusation, and ultimately the story was retracted. Jack was able to get on with the business of politics.

In the meantime, Senator Lyndon Johnson took the lead in speaking out about the space race, faulting President Eisenhower for his baby-steps approach. Johnson advocated giant steps to outshine the Soviets, and by doing so he became the Senate's leading voice on space issues. Johnson set up a new Senate subcommittee dedicated to aeronautical and space science, and he served as chairman. He felt it was time for greater federal organization to be applied to satellites, rockets, and space exploration in general. The subcommittee immediately began to plan a new space agency that would pull expertise from the various military services but remain civilian-run.

Kennedy spent most of his time in 1958 campaigning, making three speeches per week on average. He didn't focus on space, except to note that the Sputnik satellites reflected "the flaunting of the Soviets of their ability to rain death on any hostile neighbor." The message was clear: The Soviet Union had the ability to deliver an atomic weapon or an inter-continental ballistic missile capable of blowing up New York City; Washington, D.C.; or Boston—and the United States needed to respond with an arms buildup of its own.

At the same time, the Army and Navy were developing rockets capable of launching satellites into space, the Navy and Air Force were working to develop the X-15, a winged, rocket-powered airplane. The X-15 was built to detach from a B-52 bomber "mothership" at an altitude of about seven miles, a pro-cess that would eliminate the need for the first stage of a rocket launch. Once released, the X-15 would use its own rocket propulsion to fly at speeds of more than 3,600 miles per hour at altitudes of up to 62 miles, the borderline of space.

Twelve test pilots were on hand during the X-15's develop-ment. One of them was Neil Armstrong, who had become one of the most respected Navy aviators during the Korean War. He had a single-minded passion for flight, having taken his first airplane ride at age six and become permanently hooked. As a child, he built airplane models and constructed a seven-foot-long wind tunnel in his parents' basement to test his creations.

He befriended a nearby amateur astronomer so he could study the stars from the man's garage roof observatory. After attending Purdue University, Armstrong became a naval aviator and test pilot. He was known for his unflappable demeanor and detached powers of observation.

For someone who, as a young man, "was immersed in, fascinated by, and dedicated to flight," Armstrong later said, "I was disappointed by the wrinkle in history that brought me along one generation late. I had missed all the great times and adventures in flight." But between 1950 and 1957, even before Sputnik, Armstrong found himself at the center of the greatest adventure he could imagine, piloting experimental jets and other advanced flying machines and coming to understand by the early 1960s that this type of military aviation was the gateway to space exploration.

The Sputnik launches changed the world. Overnight, mankind knew that it had a future in space, and soon the media began to discuss the technological possibility of a moonshot.

For the Soviets, the launches were a public relations win and probably their greatest achievement of the Cold War. With no United Nations protests in response to the launches, the satellites set a precedent in international law that opened space to exploration. For Eisenhower, that was Sputnik's major upside: While the Soviets had beaten the U.S. to space, their satellites' use of America's high-altitude airspace gave the United States the reciprocal right to explore the Soviets' own high-altitude airspace. This played into Eisenhower's "Open Skies" idea that the best use for space was peaceful scientific research and satellite communications.

But those best uses weren't the only ones the administration was exploring. In February 1958, Eisenhower approved the CIA's top secret CORONA program, which involved the development of spy satellites capable of letting U.S. intelligence agencies know exactly where Soviet missiles were positioned.

Such reconnaissance wasn't just the province of satellites, either. Between 1956 and 1960, high-altitude U-2 spy planes conducted numerous missions over Soviet territory, photographing everything from military bases and atomic power facilities to rocket launch compounds. The U-2 program showed the kind of thinking that had made Eisenhower a success as D-Day's supreme allied commander, but its secrecy meant that it didn't earn him any immediate public credit or political points. Eisenhower was exploring the use of advanced space and near-space technology, but most people didn't know about it.

chapter eleven

Closing the Gap

B y the winter of 1958, both the Army and Navy rocket programs were so eager for success that there was a traffic jam on the Cape Canaveral launchpad. The Navy's Vanguard team had a launch of the TV3BU scheduled for February 3. Wernher von Braun wanted the Army team to beat the Navy, so he scheduled his own test on January 31, 1958.

Von Braun knew his Redstone Jupiter-C rocket was ready to go. With little fanfare, at 10:48 p.m., the firing ring was pulled and the Jupiter-C rose from the Earth, exactly as planned, roaring through the sky and disappearing into the upper atmosphere. The stages fell away on cue, leaving America's first orbiting satellite—Explorer 1—circling the Earth.

At 1:00 a.m. on February 1, two hours after the launch, von Braun announced the news to a sleepy group of reporters. The secretary of the Army and Army chief of staff congratulated von Braun and celebrated the launch as a great American achievement. Speaking for all the scientists who had come to America from Germany, von Braun said, "It makes us feel that we paid back part of the debt of gratitude we owe this country."

The next morning, the media cheered the success of Explorer 1, bringing relief and delight to millions of Americans. Most major U.S. newspapers suggested that the Explorer was the first step to American space supremacy. Even Eisenhower was thrilled, repeating the word "wonderful" three times when told of the success. He even admitted, "I sure feel a lot better now."

The Navy's Vanguard mission didn't go as well. Three days after the Explorer launch, the Navy's Vanguard TV3BU exploded in midair long before reaching space. While it was a disappointment to the Navy, in the wake of Explorer's success, most Americans didn't pay much attention. The Army was now beating the Navy in the launching of rockets.

The Explorer satellite wasn't very sophisticated or large—Soviet Premier Khrushchev called it the "grapefruit satellite" because it was only 6.4 inches in diameter—but it was mighty. While both Sputniks disintegrated when they reentered Earth's atmosphere a few months after launch, Explorer remaining in orbit until 1970, having completed more than 58,000 orbits.

That February, encouraged by success of the Explorer but still unsure of America's commitment to space, Congress followed up on Lyndon Johnson's subcommittee by establishing the Senate Special Committee on Space and Aeronautics, with the goal of establishing a new civilian space agency. Later in 1958, Congress created the Advanced Research Projects Agency to coordinate research on satellites and other space projects. The agency would oversee existing research and sponsor scientific work in business and academia.

The Advanced Research Projects Agency started the Man-in-Space-Soonest or MISS program. The $133 million program came up with an eleven-step plan, with each step representing the development and launch of a more refined and sophisticated space vehicle. The basic plans were debated, scientists were hired, and astronauts were recruited. While the program was eventually abandoned, it did accomplish three important things: It identified the goal of a manned flight to the moon with safe return, it provided a framework for achieving that goal, and it generated a list of possible astronauts.

By the summer of 1958, the agency had come up with nine names for its astronaut list, all of them high-altitude test pilots with the compact, light physiques deemed necessary for the confines of a rocket. With this lineup, MISS put faces on the American test pilots who would conquer space.

At first Eisenhower hadn't been convinced of the need for Americans to journey into outer space, but the six months since Sputnik had forced him to change his mind. The public wanted not only to go into outer space but also to beat the Soviets in getting there—in person. The president eventually came around and supported the idea of peaceful, scientific manned

President Dwight D. Eisenhower deserves credit for establishing NASA in 1958. It inherited the large organization that already existed with the NACA, and a workforce of more than 8,000 people.

space exploration. Although it angered the top Army, Navy, and Air Force leaders, Eisenhower agreed that the new space agency should be run by civilians so that other countries would be more likely to recognize it as a nonmilitary program.

On April 2, 1958, President Eisenhower spoke before Congress in support of the creation of the National Aeronautics and Space Administration (NASA), which would take over and redefine the mission for the National Advisory Committee for Aeronautics (NACA) in Hampton, Virginia. Senator Lyndon Johnson embraced Eisenhower's program. He cosponsored the Senate version of the NASA bill, and he agreed with the president that the program should be under civilian rather than military control.

Ultimately, the country's mission in space was divided between NASA and the military. NASA's work was defined as "exercising control over aeronautical and space activities sponsored by the United States," while the military continued to control "activities peculiar to or primarily associated with the development of weapons systems, military operations, or the defense of the United States." Eisenhower signed the legislation creating NASA on July 29, 1958.

Kennedy continued to use the issue of space exploration as a way to attack President Eisenhower. In a speech in April 1958, he said that "Americans were no longer the paramount power in arms, aid, trade, or appeal to the underdeveloped world." Kennedy insisted that the United States needed to create a space program that would be better than what the Soviet Union had.

At the same time Kennedy was delivering his anti-Eisenhower campaign speeches, the Congressional Joint Committee on Defense Production issued an influential report, "Deterrence & Survival in the Nuclear Age," which offered Eisenhower advice on how to deal with the Soviet Union following Sputnik. The report called for a tougher stance with Moscow, more money for military research and missile development, and increased conventional forces. It recommended the development of a second-strike force that would respond if the United States was hit by an intercontinental ballistic missile.

Kennedy embraced the report and used it often on the campaign trail. He said that the United States and its allies had little reliable information about the Soviet military's technological strengths and weaknesses. Without a clear idea of what kinds of weapons the Soviets had, the United States imagined the worst.

On August 14, 1958, in a speech on the floor of the U.S. Senate, Kennedy said, "Our nation could have afforded, and can afford now, the steps necessary to close the missile gap." The term "missile gap" caught on and became a central theme in Kennedy's senate reelection campaign. He reported that the Soviets had hundreds of intercontinental ballistic missiles while the United States didn't have a single one.

Was that true? Kennedy's remarks helped trigger a debate between the Air Force and the Central Intelligence Agency about how many missiles the Soviets actually had. Air Force analysts backed Kennedy's argument that the Soviets had stockpiles of missiles. The CIA disagreed, insisting they had less than a dozen. Declassified documents later showed that the CIA was right: At the time in question, the Soviets had only four missiles and in fact were a little behind the United States in intercontinental ballistic missile development. Soviet secrecy made it difficult for Americans to know or trust the actual risk facing the country.

NASA officially opened its doors on October 1, 1958. It had 8,000 employees, an annual budget of $100 million, and a main office in a Washington, D.C., townhouse. Several other federal labs were also brought under NASA's authority, including the Langley Aeronautical Laboratory in Virginia, the Ames Research Center in San Francisco, and the Lewis Flight Propulsion Laboratory in Cleveland, Ohio.

The NASA team got right to work. On October 11, little more than a week after its founding, NASA launched Pioneer 1, a three-stage rocket carrying instruments to measure cosmic radiation between the Earth and the moon and to collect information about the lunar surface. Unfortunately, Pioneer 1 failed to establish its orbit around the moon and plunged back into the Earth's atmosphere after forty-three hours.

President Eisenhower may not have wanted to join the space race, but the creation of NASA kicked that race into high gear. By the fall of 1958, the U.S. had launched four orbiting satellites to the Soviet Union's three, and the American satellites orbited at a higher altitude than their Soviet counterparts. An article in the *New York Times* on October 5, 1958, said, "The balance sheet of a year of effort since Sputnik I would seem to indicate that the United States was not as far behind at the time of the launching of the first satellite as was then imagined."

The Soviets enjoyed an early advantage because their space-related activities were organized by the central government in Moscow. But the Kremlin didn't realize what an advantage open-society capitalism would be to America's new space agency. NASA benefited from a connected network of industrial contractors that had invested in the development of long-range missiles even before NASA's creation. Other private businesses were eager to get involved.

To close out 1958, NASA launched Pioneer 3—the first U.S. satellite to reach an altitude of 63,580 miles—and the Air Force achieved the first long-distance flight of an intercontinental ballistic missile, which traveled more than 6,300 miles. Three weeks later, an American rocket carried a communications relay satellite into orbit. Known as SCORE (Signal Communications by Orbiting Relay Equipment), that satellite broadcast a tape recording of President Eisenhower's Christmas message to the world: the first human voice sent from space.

The development that gave the U.S. its greatest edge over the Soviets came through a private company. Working separately, electrical engineers Jack Kilby of Texas Instruments and Robert Noyce of Fairchild Semiconductor invented the microchip, which combined separate components into a single small "chip" of semiconductor material. This tiny, integrated circuit would lead to the development of portable, efficient, and affordable high-speed systems that revolutionized telecommunications technologies both on Earth and in space.

Only three months after NASA began operations, it announced the launch of Project Mercury, a program designed to put an American astronaut into space within three years. In preparing for manned spaceflight, NASA modified Navy jet-aircraft suits for surviving conditions in space, lining the inside with neoprene-coated nylon and the outside with aluminized nylon. The silver suits could provide oxygen, regulate temperature, permit movement, power communications, and shield against solar radiation.

NASA received hundreds of applications from people who wanted to become astronauts. Some of the men from the earlier Man-in-Space-Soonest list were no longer available, two because they were now over forty and considered too old, and one who'd died in a test flight accident. One of the best-known new applicants was John Glenn, a Korean War hero from Ohio. In 1941, when the United States entered World War II, Glenn had left college to join the armed forces. He worked with the Army Air Corps, Naval Aviation, and finally joined the Marines, where he became a fighter pilot in the Pacific. During the Korean War, he flew Panther jets for the Marines before moving to the Air Force, where he began flying transonic F-96 Sabre fighter jets.

He returned home a highly decorated aviation hero who was able to fly the most advanced aircraft in the United States.

After leaving the military, Glenn applied to test pilot school at the Naval Air Station Patuxent River in Maryland, although he still hadn't finished college. With strong recommendations he was accepted with the understanding that he would take extra courses at local colleges to make up classes. He learned aeronautical engineering, and after finishing the program took a job in Washington examining airplane designs. Hearing talk about a proposed cross-country flight to stress-test a new supersonic jet, Glenn volunteered and was accepted. On July 16, 1957, he flew from California to New York at record speed, arriving 3 hours, 23 minutes, and 8.4 seconds after takeoff. When NASA began accepting applications for its first astronaut class at the end of 1958, Glenn thought he was in a pretty good position to join. After all, it was common knowledge among Navy aviators that if something went wrong with an aircraft's controls, or if the wind didn't cooperate on final approach, Glenn was the best man to land safely.

While NASA worked on its list of astronauts, Kennedy prepared for Election Day 1958 by campaigning across the country. While he was running for reelection as a Massachusetts senator, he spent two-thirds of his time in other states or in Washington, D.C. He knew that his stature as a national figure made him a stronger advocate for his home state. Other members of his campaign staff spoke on his behalf when Kennedy couldn't attend an event himself. The senator coasted to a second term with 74 percent of the vote.

Kennedy essentially started campaigning for the 1960 presidential race as soon as he won reelection to the Senate. He had become a polished politician, no longer arriving to give a

Senator John F. Kennedy during his 1960 campaign for the U.S. presidency.

speech and tucking in his shirt on the way to the stage. He was confident and comfortable with himself. He now called himself JFK in a nod to president Franklin Delano Roosevelt, who'd been popularly known as FDR.

When it came to NASA, Kennedy's view was clear: no more Soviet "firsts" in space. Kennedy backed a bigger and better-funded NASA. He was proud of all that America had achieved in space by early 1959, including the launch of communication and weather satellites and of Pioneer 4, which in March had made the first successful flyby of the moon by a United States spacecraft. These were important steps toward getting an American astronaut into space.

Kennedy knew that in terms of global prestige, NASA astronauts were going to be seen as knights or cadets of American exceptionalism. Most people weren't going to care if progress was made by civilians at NASA or generals in the military. What people would care about was that America had pioneered space travel, proving that democratic capitalism was superior to state-run communism. It wasn't just conquering space that Kennedy cared about, but also winning.

chapter twelve

Mercury Seven to the Rescue

On April 9, 1959, America was introduced to the "Mercury Seven," the brave astronauts chosen to represent the United States in space. Before a packed press briefing in Washington, D.C., a curtain opened to reveal the seven astronauts, all wearing civilian clothing. NASA Administrator T. Keith Glennan made the introductions. "It is my pleasure to introduce to you," he said, "Malcolm S. Carpenter, Leroy G. Cooper, John H. Glenn Jr., Virgil I. Grissom, Walter M. Schirra Jr., Alan B. Shepard Jr., and Donald K. Slayton . . . the nation's Mercury Astronauts!"

The handsome astronauts—three from the Air Force (Cooper, Grissom, Slayton), three Navy (Carpenter, Schirra, Shepard), and one Marine (Glenn)—became overnight heroes. They were remarkably similar: all aged between thirty-two

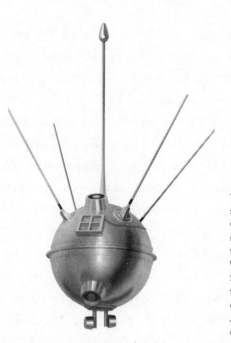

The first Soviet artificial satellite was launched on October 4, 1957, frightening many Americans into believing that they were losing the Cold War. On January 2, 1959, the Soviets launched Luna 1 (left), the first spacecraft to pass close to the moon, to Senator John F. Kennedy's great consternation.

(Cooper) and thirty-seven (Glenn), all shorter than five feet eleven inches, all white, and all male. All were seasoned test pilots, knew aircraft mechanics inside out, felt passionately about beating the Soviets, and had the mental and physical stamina to handle zero gravity. They had also survived a series of endurance tests, which included swallowing a two-foot rubber hose, nighttime parachuting, stationary bicycling past the point of exhaustion, and having spurts of frigid water shot into their eardrums at ten-second intervals.

America went astronaut crazy. Barely a week went by without a major story praising the Mercury Seven, or the

"Magnificent Seven" as they were often called by the press. America took pride not only in its astronauts, but also in the openness of NASA compared to the secrecy of the Soviet space program. As James Reston of the *New York Times* enthused, "What made them so exciting was not that they said anything new but that they said all the old things with such fierce conviction. . . . They spoke of 'duty' and 'faith' and 'country' like poet Walt Whitman's pioneers. Nobody went away from these young men scoffing at their courage or idealism."

The media attention also brought renewed interest in the life and legacy of Dr. Robert Goddard, whose patented inventions had been used in designing a number of American rockets. Though Goddard had died in 1945, his contributions to rocket science were still relevant to the space program. On May 1, 1959, the NASA facility in Beltsville, Maryland, was named the Goddard Space Flight Center in his honor.

Wernher von Braun and his team were thrilled about Project Mercury. While NASA officials thought of the Mercury Seven astronauts as test pilots, von Braun saw them as field scientists exploring outer space. "Man is still the best computer that we can put aboard a spacecraft," said von Braun. But he also knew the astronauts would need to be supported by technology that did not yet exist. For example, the support team on the ground would need a way to communicate with the astronauts as they circled the Earth. To solve this problem, NASA developed a computer that could receive signals from all over the world using satellites in space. It would become the nerve center of Project Mercury communications.

The Soviet Union continued making progress, too. On January 2, 1959, the Soviets' Luna 1 spacecraft launched on a trajectory intended to hit the moon. A malfunction caused it to miss by 3,600 miles, but Soviets defined the mission a success because it was the first time a human-made object escaped the Earth's gravity and began to orbit the sun. Nine months later, on September 14, the 3,000-pound Luna 2 succeeded where the Luna 1 had failed, crash-landing on the moon and becoming the first man-made object to connect with another planetary body.

In mid-August 1959, a month before the Luna 2 launch, the U.S. sent up the Explorer 6 satellite, which sent back the first photograph of Earth from space. Two months later, the Soviet Luna 3 took the first photographs of the far side of the moon.

Progress was also being made in the laboratory. Von Braun had developed a Saturn rocket whose first stage could deliver one and a half million pounds of thrust. That still wasn't enough for a possible American moonshot, but it showed von Braun was on his way to developing the rocket that eventually would have that honor: the Saturn V.

In Washington, the Eisenhower administration remained fairly unenthusiastic about space travel, and Kennedy continued to criticize the president and his supporters for being behind the times. President Eisenhower may have been content slow-walking into the future, but Kennedy wanted to blast forward toward a bold American victory in space. Though not yet saying directly that America would put an astronaut on the moon by 1970, Kennedy boasted that if he were made president, the United States would be first in space.

chapter thirteen

Kennedy for President

When John F. Kennedy formally announced his candidacy for president of the United States on January 2, 1960, he promised that he would elevate the stature of American science and education. NASA welcomed the news, hoping that Kennedy would prioritize NASA funding.

Time magazine called Kennedy "a serious man on a serious mission." His visionary ideas about innovation and technology stood in contrast with the more conservative approach of the likely Republican nominee, Vice President Richard Nixon. Kennedy was always eager to point out these differences while on the campaign trial.

Kennedy also had support from his family. To make campaigning easier, Kennedy's father bought him a Convair 240 twin-engine airplane. Named *Caroline* after his two-year-old daughter, the plane helped him cover some 100,000 miles during the campaign. It gave him an edge over his political rivals, letting him set his own itinerary based on political benefit rather than on train and airline schedules.

Kennedy's major rivals for the Democratic nomination were Senate colleagues Stuart Symington of Missouri, Hubert Humphrey of Minnesota, and Lyndon Johnson of Texas. Kennedy understood politics, and he always tried to maximize his political strength. Sometimes that meant making uncomfortable compromises. For example, Senator Symington refused to speak to racially segregated audiences in the South, while Kennedy was willing to look the other way in order to win votes. He didn't want to lose the segregated Southern states over civil rights, so he didn't overly emphasize racial issues as a candidate.

He tried to present himself in a way that would appeal to as many voters as possible. The most conservative voters were satisfied with Kennedy's anti-Soviet "missile gap" tough talk, while more liberal voters could get behind his defense of Social Security and other New Deal programs. Kennedy hired smart people to work as his personal assistants and aides. He came off as cool, genuine, and comfortable around people. He was a natural campaigner—articulate and willing to speak anywhere, with a picture-perfect family and no trouble raising money.

"Jack was always out kissing babies, while I was passing bills," Lyndon Johnson complained, and he had a point:

Kennedy's lack of a strong legislative record was his biggest liability during the 1960 campaign. But Kennedy wasn't a lightweight; he was a driven man on a mission. Johnson, Humphrey, and Symington might have been better senators, but Kennedy was the better presidential candidate.

As 1960 began, NASA was still trying to get its footing. Von Braun, who had moved with the other Huntsville rocket engineers from the Army to NASA, went to his new bosses and pushed for support of his ambitious plan to go to the moon in a three-stage rocket. The NASA director promised that the rocket programs in Huntsville would be funded, but von Braun did not get the pledge of support he wanted.

The idea of NASA planning a moon mission before humans had sent an astronaut into space sounded too much like a reckless Cold War competition for NASA Director T. Keith Glennan. Like President Eisenhower, he preferred for NASA to make progress slowly and methodically rather than rushing to be first.

This measured approach annoyed Kennedy, especially during election season. He wanted bolder action in space, and considered Project Mercury as just the beginning of America's efforts. He thought bold steps in space would bring breakthroughs in science and technology that would usher in an era of American technological superiority, progress, and national prosperity. While some criticized the space race, Kennedy embraced it. He saw the benefit of aiming for the stars.

• • •

The perception of the United States as technologically behind the Soviets changed almost overnight on May 1, 1960, when the public learned that an American U-2 spy plane had been shot down in Soviet airspace. The U-2 was a top secret, ultra-high-altitude single-jet aircraft able to gather intelligence day or night from an elevation of 70,000 feet, well on the way to space. These planes flew so high that pilots needed to wear partially pressurized suits that delivered oxygen, much like astronauts' space suits. U.S. pilot Francis Gary Powers was taking spy photos when the Soviets detected his plane and fired three surface-to-air missiles in his direction, one of which caused Powers to crash.

Eisenhower assumed Powers had not survived the accident. The White House first tried to cover up the U-2's mission, putting out a press release claiming that the pilot, on a weather-gathering mission over Turkey, had become sick due to oxygen deprivation and crashed in Soviet territory.

The story changed when Soviet Premier Nikita Khrushchev reported that Powers had in fact survived and been captured by the Soviets, who had also recovered part of his U-2. Eisenhower was forced to admit guilt, and Powers was convicted of spying.

The incident increased the tension between the United States and the Soviet Union. But it also showed that the United States was not only keeping up with but perhaps even exceeding Soviet technology. NASA engineers cheered the military's

The launch of the Freedom 7 mission at Cape Canaveral, Florida, on May 5, 1961. Alan Shepard, the sole occupant of the capsule, became the first American in space. His flight lasted only fifteen minutes.

Project Mercury astronauts trying on space gear, including pressure suits, in 1959. Clockwise from left: unidentified technician, Donald "Deke" Slayton, John Glenn, Scott Carpenter, Leroy Gordon Cooper, Virgil "Gus" Grissom, Alan Shepard (in helmet), technician, Wally Schirra, technician

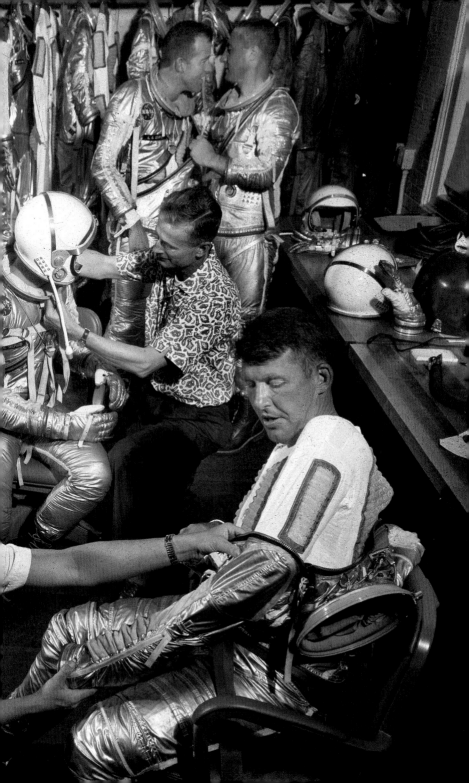

Above: Engineers working through the night in 1963 at NASA's assembly center near Edwards Air Force Base in Kern County, California.

Right: On February 23, 1962, President Kennedy visited Cape Canaveral to honor John Glenn, who three days before became the first American to orbit the earth. He was photographed receiving a personal tour of Glenn's Friendship 7 space capsule. Kennedy and Glenn would become warm friends, apart from their towering roles in national events.

Above: Like the other Mercury astronauts, Gus Grissom trained on a multiple-axis machine specially built to replicate and even exceed the amount of spinning actually encountered in space travel.

Right: On July 16, 1969, almost six years after John F. Kennedy's death, the 35th U.S. president's dream of an American voyage to the moon came to fruition. Apollo 11 brought together the talents of many thousands of workers but carried only three on the mission: Neil Armstrong, Buzz Aldrin, and Michael Collins. The photograph shows the Saturn V rocket that propelled the Apollo 11 astronauts into space. Four days later, on July 20, Armstrong and Aldrin took the most daring step of all, climbing into the tiny Eagle lunar module and detaching from the command module, on which Collins remained. The spiderlike Eagle then made its way to the surface of the moon.

Above: "The Eagle has landed," Armstrong reported to Houston's Apollo Mission Control at 4:18 p.m. on July 20, 1969. After six hours of further preparations and mandatory rest, Armstrong climbed down a ladder and set foot on the moon, saying, "That's one small step for [a] man, one giant leap for mankind."

Right: After more than twenty-one hours on the moon, the Eagle successfully lifted off and approached the command module. The complex docking procedure was completed, reuniting the three astronauts for the journey home to Earth. Only after their safe arrival on July 24 could the Apollo 11 mission be fully celebrated as the historic accomplishment that it was.

triumph in producing an aeronautical marvel like the U-2. Though the Mercury project was years away from putting an American in space, planning was already under way for a follow-up program that would attempt to launch a three-man team with the new Saturn rocket.

In 1959, with von Braun's Jupiter missiles being deployed in Western Europe, he focused on Saturn, his new rocket program. His reason for picking the name was simple: Saturn "was the next outer planet in the solar system." But when it came time for NASA to name its next flight program, it went in a different direction. Dr. Abe Silverstein, NASA's chief of space flight programs, had named Project Mercury after the messenger of the Roman gods. Sticking with Greco-Roman mythology as inspiration for the name of the mission that followed Mercury, he suggested Apollo, for the god of music, medicine, prophecy, light, and progress. "I thought the image of the god Apollo riding his chariot across the sun gave the best representation of the grand scale of the proposed program," said Dr. Silverstein.

In 1960, NASA made the name Apollo official. This mission would include carrying astronauts to a space station, orbiting the moon, and eventually making a manned lunar landing.

In July 1960, Jack Kennedy headed to the Democratic National Convention in Los Angeles. Even those who didn't like Kennedy had to admit he had run a flawless, media-savvy campaign. The tension between Kennedy and Lyndon Johnson turned ugly at the convention. There were rumors that Kennedy had said that Johnson's 1955 heart attack made him unfit for the White House. Johnson struck back, telling a reporter at the *Chicago Daily News* that Jack was a "little scrawny fellow with rickets" who suffered from Addison's disease and took regular injections of cortisone. The accusations were mean, but not inaccurate. Kennedy's team responded by criticizing Johnson for unfairly attacking the PT-109 hero. Ultimately, Johnson was forced to apologize.

Kennedy was chosen as the Democratic nominee for president. In an attempt to balance the ticket and heal the differences with Johnson, Kennedy chose the Texan as his vice-presidential running mate. In personality, education, religion, style, region, and expertise, the two were opposites, so ill-paired that Republican presidential nominee Richard Nixon called the relationship "an uneasy and joyless marriage of convenience."

In his acceptance speech at the Democratic Convention, Kennedy declared that the "New Frontier" had arrived. Unlike the New Deal, his administration wouldn't focus on the government helping people, but rather on people helping the United States achieve new greatness. "The New Frontier of which I speak is not a set of promises," Kennedy said. "It is a set of challenges. It sums up not what I intend to offer the American people, but what I intend to ask of them. It appeals to their pride, not their pocketbook—it holds out the promise of more sacrifice instead of more security."

On purpose, the New Frontier was flexible in meaning,

more of an attitude of winning the future than a specific series of problems. Whatever the New Frontier would be, it seemed anchored, in part, around a new age of space exploration. The Mercury Seven astronauts were relatively young. Kennedy was the youthful, independent-minded leader of a new generation that was starting to dominate an American society just waking from the prosperous sleep of the Eisenhower years. Kennedy and his team offered self-possession, glamour, celebrity, patriotism, and a hunger for enhanced global prestige.

In this forward-looking time of national reflection, science and space were crowd-pleasers. These themes continued to play when the Republicans nominated Richard Nixon—also a NASA supporter—at their convention in Chicago a few weeks later, with Henry Cabot Lodge Jr. (Kennedy's former Senate opponent from Massachusetts) as his running mate. Though both major party tickets favored space exploration, Kennedy claimed the upper hand by arguing that the United States had lost its lead due to Eisenhower's and Nixon's weak leadership.

Kennedy talked about the "space gap" and "missile gap" throughout the campaign. In late July, the director of the CIA grew so frustrated with this that he called Kennedy and Johnson in for a classified intelligence briefing. He shared information gathered from U-2 spy missions and on-the-ground intelligence, proving that the missile gap was a Cold War myth. In fact, the United States was considerably ahead of its enemy.

After the briefing, Kennedy simply chose to disregard the

evidence and continue hammering the missile gap argument for political reasons. Nixon and Lodge had received the same briefing following their nomination, and they were enraged. They knew Kennedy was knowingly misrepresenting the truth, but they couldn't call him out because the CIA information they'd received was highly classified.

Kennedy kept at it. On the campaign trial, he used the space and missile gaps to demonstrate how American technology in general had fallen behind the Soviets during the Eisenhower era. "The people of the world respect achievement," Kennedy said to a crowd on September 7. "For most of the twentieth century they admired American science and American education, which were second to none. But they are not at all certain about which way the future lies."

Nixon defended the Eisenhower administration's technological accomplishments by celebrating the successful 1959 launch of Echo 1, a one-hundred-foot, inflatable aluminized balloon satellite that bounced television and radio beams off its surface to facilitate long-range communications. But the success of Echo 1 was overshadowed by the Soviet launch of Korabl-Sputnik 2, which carried canine passengers Belka and Strelka into orbit and returned them safely to Earth.

Beyond space and missiles, the campaign was also defined by other issues. Voters who didn't like Kennedy questioned his fitness for office because of his religion. Some in the Republican Party argued that a Catholic in the White House wouldn't support America's constitutional separation of church and state, suggesting that he would put the interests of the Vatican above those of his own country. The Minnesota Baptist Convention went so far as to declare that both Catholicism and communism were serious threats to America.

Kennedy responded by pointing out that nobody had cared about his religion when he served in the U.S. Navy during World War II. Brushing aside the religion issue, he turned visionary, saying that he saw an America "with too many slums, with too few schools, and too late to the moon and outer space." The speech was televised and proved to be a turning point in the campaign.

In speeches around the country, Kennedy spoke of leadership being about boldness and daring for greatness. "I am tired of reading every morning what Mr. Khrushchev is doing," Kennedy said. "I want to read what the president of the United States is doing."

During a series of four televised debates—the first in U.S. history—both the Democratic and Republican candidates promised a new political era and a sharp turn from Eisenhower's methodical style, but Kennedy seemed to be the real embodiment of change. Nixon came off as an old-style politician, while Kennedy appealed to voters who wanted a man of action with the vision to move the country forward. "I look up and see the Soviet flag on the moon," Kennedy goaded Nixon at the October 21 debate. "Polls on our prestige and influence around the world have shown such a sharp drop that up until now the State Department had been unwilling to release them."

The four televised Kennedy-Nixon debates of October 1960 were watched by millions of Americans. On October 21, the upstart Kennedy chided Vice President Nixon that the United States was losing the space race to Khrushchev. "I look up and see the Soviet flag on the moon. Polls on our prestige and influence around the world have shown such a sharp drop that up till now the State Department has been unwilling to release them."

On Election Day, polls showed Kennedy and Nixon in a tie. The votes were counted into the night. Eventually, Kennedy won the election with 303 electoral votes to Nixon's 219, and a slim 0.1 percent lead in the popular vote. NASA Director Glennan knew that Kennedy would want his own man to lead NASA. That November, Glennan briefed Kennedy's transition team on Project Mercury. The president-elect didn't wait long to make his mark on America's space agency.

Part III
MOONBOUND

chapter fourteen

Setting the Course at NASA

Inauguration Day, January 18, 1960, dawned with an icy wind ripping through the nation's capital. The ground was covered in snow from the previous night, but right on cue, the sun shone down and warmed the crowd as John F. Kennedy took the oath of office as the thirty-fifth president of the United States.

The youngest man ever elected to the White House, Kennedy looked vibrant as he stood to give his inaugural address. "Let the word go forth from this time and place, to friend and foe alike," he said, "that the torch has been passed to a new generation of Americans—born in this century, tempered by war, disciplined by a hard and bitter peace, proud of our ancient heritage—and unwilling to witness or permit the slow undoing of those human rights to which this nation has always been committed, and to which we are committed today at home and around the world."

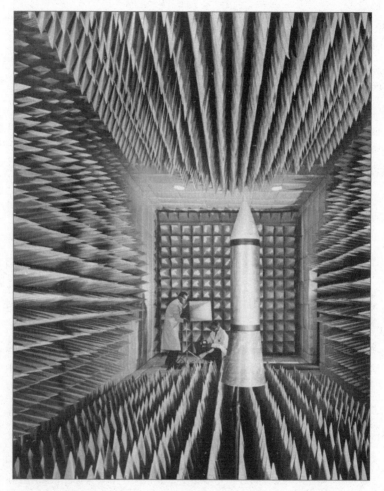

Space and ballistic missile technology became the rage in the 1950s and 1960s. Here radar echoes are absorbed in an anechoic chamber so that engineers can ricochet echoless beams off the nose cone of a ICBM prototype.

The speech thrilled and motivated the nation, urging a new sense of national service and sacrifice. Later he delivered one of the speech's most memorable lines: "Ask not what your country can do for you, ask what you can do for your country."

With the campaign behind him, Kennedy now faced responsibility for fixing the problems of the nation. He had focused on the missile gap with the Soviets, but in February 1961, the president's own defense study concluded that there was no missile gap. In fact, the opposite was true: When President Eisenhower left the White House, the United States had one hundred and sixty intercontinental ballistic missiles and the Soviet Union had only four.

The report confirmed that Eisenhower had actually done a great job of building up United States defenses. When Eisenhower became president in 1952, the Air Force still used piston-driven bombers. By the time Kennedy took office, the United States had developed spy satellites, nuclear submarines, and a fleet of 1,500 jet bombers capable of dropping hydrogen bombs. America had not let the sophisticated Soviets dominate the skies.

Kennedy did, however, see a real gap in global prestige. That's why manned space travel still mattered. He thought putting an American astronaut in space would provide a publicity windfall, and it would help the United States lead from a position of strength. The new president wanted to stop the Soviets from claiming any more Sputnik-like public relations victories, but when he came into office, Kennedy had no clear plan on how to change NASA to speed its progress.

Before he was sworn in, Kennedy formed an urgent task force to prepare a report with recommendations for NASA's future. On January 10, 1961, the committee submitted its report, which surprised by recommending against manned space exploration. The report said that Project Mercury was of exaggerated value to the United States and should be discontinued. The authors argued that the race to hurry into space could lead to mission failure and loss of life. The Mercury Seven astronauts worried that they had just completed a grueling, year-long training for nothing. No one knew the future of the manned space program.

Another of the report's recommendations was the replacement of NASA director T. Keith Glennan with someone who would focus on the nonmilitary aspects of space exploration. This proved a challenge. Many qualified candidates weren't interested in taking over a brand-new government agency that was in transition and lacked a clear vision for its future. Seventeen candidates turned down the post. The eighteenth also wanted to decline, but President Kennedy personally urged him to take on the responsibility, telling him he'd have the power to shape NASA in dramatic ways. James Webb eventually agreed to serve, and he proved to be the ideal choice.

Webb was a respected North Carolina lawyer who wasn't a scientist or rocket expert but did understand policy and how to manage big government budgets. He had a reassuring personality that put people at ease. He had worked in private industry, supplying a flight navigation system to the armed forces, and he knew a lot of leaders in the aeronautics business. Webb was a smart man with a rare combination of business knowledge, bipartisan political instincts, networking skills between academia and big business, and personal charm. He had also served as a U.S. Marine.

Many in the space program worried that Webb would follow the recommendations of the task force and end manned space missions. But after he took over on February 14, 1961, he immediately calmed NASA's 19,000 employees by reassuring them that the agency remained firmly committed to manned space missions.

Under Webb's leadership, NASA soon emerged as one of the most efficient and effective government agencies of the 1960s. At a March budget meeting, Webb explained to Kennedy that the manned program had to continue. The Soviets were preparing to launch a man into space. With the game of sending humans beyond Earth's atmosphere already well along, the public would be enraged if Kennedy threw in the towel. Webb argued that the space program was a global advertisement for American technical know-how, and that it would also benefit the military and society in general by producing valuable spin-off technologies. Webb recommended to Kennedy that the NASA budget be increased by more than $300 million, an amount that would allow it to fast-track the Saturn booster rocket program, with the goal of sending

American astronauts to the moon.

Kennedy agreed with Webb's every word. He knew that the space race with the Soviets was a challenge to the American way of life. And Americans, he knew, could be motivated by that challenge to rise to greatness. Putting an astronaut in space—perhaps even on the moon—would be good for the spirit of the nation. Together, Webb and Kennedy were ready to lead the nation on a great adventure.

chapter fifteen

The First Men in Space

E arly in his presidency, John F. Kennedy wasn't sure which issues to fight for first. That changed on April 12, 1961, when Russian cosmonaut Yuri Gagarin became the first human to go to outer space. During his 108-minute journey, Gagarin completed a single low orbit and returned safely to Earth.

Gagarin was photogenic, smart, fearless, and physically fit. An outgoing Russian Air Force major, he became the top cosmonaut of the Soviet space program. Soviet Premier Nikita Khrushchev knew that the mission would drive Soviet global prestige even higher, and Gagarin would take his place with ocean navigators like Ferdinand Magellan and Christopher Columbus in the annals of human exploration.

The rocket used to launch Gagarin's spacecraft was similar to that used to launch Sputnik. Fearing that zero gravity in

On April 12, 1961, Russian cosmonaut Yuri Gagarin became the first human in outer space. President John F. Kennedy was embarrassed that the Soviet feat took place on his White House watch. It helped spur his decision to back a U.S. effort to go to the moon.

outer space might cause the cosmonaut to become light-headed or incoherent, the Soviets designed the space capsule to be piloted by engineers on the ground. While the Soviets had worked out the launch, they hadn't figured out how to have Gagarin return inside the spacecraft. When it was time to return to Earth, Gagarin ejected from the capsule about four miles in the air, then parachuted safely into a farmer's field. The capsule simply crashed into the ground. NASA engineers noticed, and considered it a telltale sign that the Kremlin was rushing to be first in manned space exploration, rather than taking time to refine its aerospace designs.

Kennedy sent a telegram to Khrushchev congratulating him on the historic achievement, but the president was shaken. When asked about the Soviet mission, Kennedy acknowledged that the United States was falling behind in space flight. "It is a fact that it is going to take some time," he said.

While Kennedy had been a longstanding critic of President Eisenhower's go-slow approach to space, in his early presidency he had adopted a similar caution. Instead of putting resources into space exploration, Kennedy had been focused on domestic economic issues, such as rising unemployment and low stock prices. With news of the Soviet success, Kennedy wanted his administration to begin working harder on space-related issues.

Kennedy knew the United States needed to get a man into space soon, so he asked the staff at NASA to work double shifts. Eisenhower's old science advisor warned Kennedy that NASA wasn't ready for a manned space mission, and that if a Mercury astronaut was launched too early, the flight would be "the most expensive funeral man has ever had." Kennedy listened, but still decided that getting an American astronaut into space had to be a White House priority.

On April 14, Kennedy met with the key space advisors in his administration. His budget director was on hand to remind the group that every dollar spent in space was a dollar taken away from domestic programs or an additional dollar that had to be raised in taxes. With that limitation in mind, Kennedy asked what the country could do to leapfrog ahead in space exploration. The next American move had to be dramatic.

However, Kennedy was immediately distracted by another urgent matter. About an hour after the space meeting broke up, a small fleet set sail from Nicaragua and Guatemala, bound for an inlet known as the Bay of Pigs, on the southern coast of Cuba. The invasion by Cuban exiles—which had been funded by the CIA—was designed to overthrow the communist government of Fidel Castro, which two years before had deposed U.S.-backed authoritarian president Fulgencio Batista after a long revolutionary struggle.

The Bay of Pigs invasion had been doomed from the start. Castro's government knew about the plan and fired on the counterrevolutionaries as soon as they began landing. Hundreds were killed on both sides, including some Americans. On its own, the invasion's failure didn't have much to do with

American space policy. But following the heels of the Soviets winning the race to put a man in space, it was a double hit to Kennedy's reputation. If he were to remain a popular president, he would have to strengthen the reputation of the United States in the world via space technology.

On April 20, Kennedy met with Vice President Lyndon Johnson and NASA director James Webb, asking their input on the best space mission to undertake next. Eight days later, Johnson told Kennedy that NASA was important in terms of international relations, noting that "dramatic accomplishments in space are being increasingly identified as a major indicator of world leadership."

After interviewing a number of experts, Johnson said that the United States was not going to get reliable information about space from any other source. "We cannot expect the Russians to transfer the benefits of their experiences or the advantages of their capacities to us," he wrote. "We must do these things ourselves." Johnson concluded that a manned trip to the moon was necessary and could be achieved by 1966 or 1967. Rocket researcher Wernher von Braun followed up a day later with a letter arguing that a moon landing was possible by 1967 or 1968.

Kennedy considered backing a trip to the moon, but in the shorter term he encouraged NASA to remain focused on its manned Mercury program, which was nearing its first planned mission. NASA responded by making the bold but risky decision to encourage television and radio coverage of their upcoming launch. This policy of openness contrasted starkly with the secrecy of the Soviet space program.

After several missed dates, a launch date of May 5 was announced for the first American astronaut to head to outer space. But tragedy struck the day before takeoff. On May 4, Lieutenant Commander Victor Prather and another scientist participated in the final test of the full-pressure Mark IV space suits the Mercury astronauts would use. As part of their experiment, they flew in a balloon to a height of 21.5 miles, then landed in the Gulf of Mexico, where a Navy helicopter was on hand to pull them out of the water. The first researcher successfully climbed onto a sling lowered from the helicopter and made his way out of the water. But it was particularly difficult to hold on because the sling had been designed for people wearing wet suits or street clothes, rather than twenty-five-pound space suits. When it was Prather's turn to climb into the helicopter, he slipped and fell into the ocean, where water poured into the face guard of his suit, which he'd opened after landing. The weight of the water in his suit pulled him under, and he drowned before Navy divers could reach him. His death gave NASA and Kennedy a stark reminder of the high risk of rushing astronauts into space too early.

The first American chosen to go into space was Alan Shepard Jr., a top-shape Navy test pilot from New Hampshire. The physically fit astronaut was known for his calm judgment, deep

On May 5, 1961, members of the Kennedy administration gathered in the White House office of the president's secretary, Evelyn Lincoln, to watch the liftoff of Alan Shepard aboard a Mercury-Redstone rocket. Left to right: Vice President Lyndon Johnson, Arthur Schlesinger Jr., Admiral Arleigh Burke, and President John F. Kennedy and First Lady Jacqueline Kennedy were thrilled when Shepard's Freedom 7 capsule successfully splashed down in the Atlantic ocean.

concentration, and rough-and-ready attitude. On the day of the launch, the takeoff time was delayed again and again by weather and mechanical problems. Millions of people watching on TV grew anxious. After four hours waiting while strapped fully suited into his module atop the seven-story rocket, Shepard kept his sense of humor. "Why don't you fix your little problem and light this candle?" he asked the control tower.

At 9:34 a.m., Eastern Standard Time, NASA finally lit the

candle. Kennedy and his wife, Jackie, watched on television as the rocket rose from the launchpad, firing Shepard into history. In all, Shepard spent 15 minutes and 28 seconds aloft, peaking at an altitude of 116.5 miles, before splashing down in the Atlantic Ocean 302 miles from Cape Canaveral. Still strapped inside the Freedom 7 module, he was successfully rescued after splashdown. Unlike Gagarin's remote-controlled flight, Shepard had piloted his Freedom 7 ship himself, proving it was possible for an astronaut to maintain hands-on control despite the high stresses and weightlessness of space flight.

Twenty-three days after the Soviet launched its first manned space flight, America had done it, too. Across the country, 45 million viewers had watched what was later called "the greatest 'suspense drama' in the history of TV." The experienced bonded the nation, bringing America together like nothing had since V-J Day at the close of World War II.

Kennedy understood that space exploration had the power to unite the nation in peacetime. After Shepard's safe return, America seemed to forget the shame of the Soviet mission. Kennedy and Shepard became friends, based on a shared willingness to take huge risks to beat the Soviets in space.

Strengthening the space program was now a New Frontier priority. Kennedy promised that the United States government would oversee a "substantially larger effort in space." Just days after Shepard's successful mission, NASA officials met with Pentagon brass to discuss the future, touching on everything from communications satellites and intercontinental ballistic missiles to Project Mercury. The open question was whether the U.S. should commit itself to landing on the moon. The group admitted that the point of a moonshot was global prestige, proving American technological excellence over the Soviets. There really weren't any direct military advantages.

Shepard was flown to Washington, D.C., where Kennedy presented him with NASA's Distinguished Service Medal. Less than two weeks later, Kennedy set up a meeting with Victor Prather's widow, Virginia, and her two small children. Kennedy posthumously awarded Prather with the Navy Distinguished Flying Cross in honor of his service and sacrifice. The American spirit had been stirred by brave men like Prather and Shepard, and Kennedy planned to build on this national feeling to increase NASA's budget.

chapter sixteen

We're Going to the Moon

On May 25, 1961, Congress assembled in a joint session to hear President John F. Kennedy's special address on "Urgent National Needs." The White House considered the afternoon speech a kind of second inaugural address, a chance for the president, just four months into his administration, to define his message to the nation.

In the six weeks between Yuri Gagarin's history-making manned space flight and Kennedy's May speech, his New Frontier vision had turned toward an American mission to the moon. From Kennedy's perspective, the unprecedented goal would be a combination of heroic journey and public relations victory, and it would provide the country with a scientific windfall, developing technologies that would kick-start greater economic progress.

President Kennedy at the joint session of Congress on May 25, 1961, making his historic American pledge: "I believe that this nation should commit itself to achieving the goal, before this decade is out, of landing a man on the moon and returning him safely to Earth."

A few days before the speech, Kennedy invited the Mercury Seven astronauts to the Oval Office, along with several White House officials devoted to the program. Kennedy asked their advice on the difficult questions he would almost certainly face from the press: Were the Mercury missions essential? Was it necessary to send a person into space, or could robots or monkeys perform as well? What would the United States gain?

At the time, many critics—including respected scientists—questioned the need for manned space flights and argued there was no need to rush to the moon. NASA could work at a steady pace and reach the lunar surface by the late 1970s or 1980s without pushing the nation's budget and capacities to their limits. But politics demanded a different timetable. Kennedy knew the moon had become the ultimate prize in America's fierce rivalry with the Soviets over technological superiority, and he wanted to claim the mantle.

Kennedy reminded his skeptics that World War II lawmakers thought the NACA (NASA's predecessor) was a waste of money, but that in fact it had developed technologies for almost every aircraft used in the war. Kennedy knew that the moon mission would have similar effects, producing dazzling new innovations that would revolutionize computer technology, telecommunications, and more, and transform society for generations to come. The possibilities could barely be imagined.

The idea wasn't without risk, though. If NASA failed, Kennedy failed. If Kennedy failed, America failed. And Kennedy knew that space launches often did fail. From 1957 to 1961, there had been two disasters for every successful rocket launch at Cape Canaveral.

No one knew the Kremlin's real abilities or intentions. A CIA report estimated that the Soviets probably could not send a human to the moon within ten years. But assuring that the

United States beat them to it would require enormous congressional funding and a committed effort by American taxpayers. Entire new computer systems and space hardware would have to be created.

Kennedy also had to deal with the fact that any money spent on the space program would take away from his other domestic priorities. In 1961, the economy was improving but it wasn't strong. The president favored U.S. government anti-poverty and civil rights programs, and Congress wanted infrastructure spending to rebuild bridges, highways, and electric utility grids. Kennedy understood that the politics of spending were tricky. Money spent on space would generate new high-paying jobs and innovations that would boost the economy, but these gains would happen over the long term and be less obvious than something like building a new road. These were difficult ideas to explain to voters.

The president was also interested in space as an issue of national defense. He worried that Soviet satellites could soon be equipped with nuclear bombs. Kennedy pushed for a ban on all nuclear weaponry in space, but the Soviets resisted. They were concerned that a ban would also limit their ability to conduct satellite surveillance.

As the United States and the Soviet Union began diplomatic negotiations toward a superpower agreement about peace in space, Kennedy asked the Air Force to stop publicizing their own military developments in space. Specifically, their X-15 rocket plane was breaking speed and altitude records for a reusable craft. Even more advanced was the Dyna-Soar, an airplane-like spacecraft that was able to enter space, orbit the Earth, and return.

The U.S. Air Force resented Kennedy's approach, which favored the Army's Huntsville program. They saw it as evidence that the president wanted to keep NASA at the center of things while relegating military space technology development to the shadows. The military worried that this approach would cause them to lose out on essential funding.

As Kennedy prepared to address Congress, a draft of a major study sponsored by the Air Force was under review. It pushed for the Air Force to take over leadership of the manned space program from the civilian-run NASA. Kennedy knew the Air Force could possibly reach the moon faster than NASA, but he worried that the approach would blur the lines about the militarization of space.

The easiest thing for Kennedy to do would have been to slowly and incrementally make progress in funding NASA's manned space program. Few in Congress expected a bold new direction for NASA. But Kennedy wasn't able to resist the temptation to advance one of the biggest scientific breakthroughs in human history. The risks were great, but so were the benefits. Kennedy was fond of a saying by the legendary aviator Amelia Earhart: "Everyone has oceans to fly, if they have the heart to do it. Is it reckless? Maybe. But what do dreams know of boundaries?"

• • •

40

64

the dramatic achievements in space
which occurred in recent weeks should
as that this proposal might aspen
have made clear to us all the impact *~iss*
new every where
of this new frontier of human
adventure. Since early in my term,
our efforts in space have been under
review. With the advice of the *and Space*
who is the Chairman of the National Committee
Vice President we have examined where
we are strong and where we are not,
where we may succeed and where we may
not. Now it is time to take longer
strides -- time for a great new
American enterprise -- time for this
nation to take a clearly leading role
in space achievement, *which in many ways*
may hold the key to our future on earth.

Reading copy of President John F. Kennedy's Special Message to Congress on "Urgent National Needs," delivered May 25, 1961. In the address, Kennedy argues for increased support of the National Aeronautics and Space Administration (NASA) and the United States' landing a man on the moon by the end of the decade.

On the morning of May 25, Kennedy was still polishing his speech. At first, he was going to declare that America would put a man on the moon by 1967—the fiftieth anniversary of the Russian Revolution of 1917—but he switched to "the end of the decade" to give NASA a bit more time. For the first hour of his speech, Kennedy discussed military spending and Soviet relations. Then he turned to space. He framed the discussion of space exploration as a choice between tyranny and freedom. Kennedy knew that conservatives would find it hard to resist supporting a trip to the moon framed as a way to prove democratic capitalism's superiority to communism.

He mentioned the Soviets' successes in building rockets and satellites, stressing that the United States had to work harder. "For while we cannot guarantee that we shall one day be first, we can guarantee that any failure to make this effort will make us last," he said. Then he laid out the grand challenge that would come to define his presidency and legacy: "I believe this nation should commit itself to achieving the goal, before the decade is out, of landing a man on the moon and returning him safely to earth."

It was one of the most courageous statements and greatest gambles ever made by an American president. Considering that NASA's total accomplishment in manned space flight to date was Alan Shepard's fifteen-minute suborbital flight three weeks before, Kennedy's decision to shoot for the moon was extra bold.

At first, his audience seemed skeptical of the moon

challenge. They didn't applaud or cheer him much. Kennedy's voice lost some of its confidence. He later wondered if he should have leaked word about the plan a week in advance so that some members of Congress and the press would have been more energized.

By the following day, the nation had caught up with Kennedy's enthusiasm, but there were concerns about the high financial cost. Some legislators complained that "our debt may reach the moon before we do," and others worried that space spending would lead to inflation. Even the president's father, Joseph Kennedy, criticized the plan. "I taught Jack better than that!" he raged. "Oh, we're going to go broke with this nonsense!"

Kennedy set out an ambitious plan, but it was up to Congress to fund it. The mission would require huge increases in the NASA budget, an issue that would be decided by a congressional vote in mid-July.

chapter seventeen

Gearing Up for a Lunar Voyage

With a track record of only one manned space flight—a fifteen-minute ride that didn't include a single trip around the planet—the United States had committed itself to leap-frogging its own capabilities and putting a man on the moon. To achieve that goal, new systems of navigation and communication would need to be invented and engineers would need to build a rocket more powerful than the eight-engine Saturn I. "The gap between a twenty-minute up-and-down flight and going to the moon was something almost beyond belief, technically," said astronaut Neil Armstrong.

America went right to work. As fate would have it, the first "Conference on Peaceful Uses of Space" had been scheduled for

May 26, 1961, the day after Kennedy announced the U.S. moon-shot. Held in Tulsa, Oklahoma, the meeting included aerospace industry leaders and engineers, all of whom were thrilled after the announcement of America's new mission.

Kennedy addressed the crowd in a three-minute telephone call, focusing on the benefits of space research and the need to maintain American leadership in the field. Oklahoma Democratic senator Robert S. Kerr, chair of the United States Senate Committee on Aeronautical and Space Sciences, also spoke to the attendees, telling them, "The costs will be tremendous, but the rewards will be unlimited."

After a day of speeches, NASA director James Webb delivered an upbeat address, arguing that the country had to go to the moon. "We have the scientists, we have the technology, we have the resources, and we have the power and knowledge to do the job," Webb said. "Not to do it would jeopardize the nation's future."

Surprisingly, the White House's own representative at the conference turned out to be a critic of the moon program. Former radio and television news broadcaster Edward R. Murrow had joined the Kennedy administration as head of the U.S. Information Agency. Only a few days before, he'd made his first public appearance in his new job, discussing the Cold War with the Soviet Union at the National Press Club in Washington, D.C. He surprised the audience there by speaking out against racial segregation in the South, lamenting that America policies meant that diplomats from African countries were forced to endure segregation while in the United States. "Landlords will not rent to them," Murrow said. "Schools refused their children." He noted that these acts of discrimination, coupled with the images of violence endured by civil rights activists in the South, were broadcast to the world and cost America "as much influence as anything the Soviets might do."

To the surprise of others in the Kennedy administration, Murrow argued that NASA was a distraction from the societal problems America faced at home. He admitted that Apollo offered hope for building national pride, but he said he wasn't as sure that the New Frontier America of outer space could coexist with America's troubled "inner spaces."

By backing the moonshot with billions of dollars, Kennedy seemed to be turning his back on the war on poverty, civil rights, education, environmental conservation, and medical research. Spending the same amount of money in any of these areas would have made a huge near-term difference in people's lives. By supporting the moonshot, Kennedy was gambling on an even bigger long-term social and economic boost, but there was also the possibility that it would all be a flop.

Kennedy was aware of these forces, but he believed in undaunted courage: Life is short, bold steps forward are immortal, so act on behalf of future generations.

NASA considered several approaches to land a man on the moon. One approach was known as direct ascent, in which a giant rocket would lift off from Earth, land on the moon, and then return. The problem was that the rocket would have to be absolutely huge to have enough power for a round-trip voyage.

A second method was Earth-orbit rendezvous. In this scheme, multiple rockets would launch one after the other, each carrying part of the spacecraft. Once they were in orbit around the Earth, the components would be affixed together. This combined ship would fly to the moon and land, then a smaller part of it would return home.

A third design was known as the lunar-orbit rendezvous (LOR) option. This approach would use a formidable three-stage rocket to launch three NASA astronauts and an assembly of three separate elements: a command module, a service module, and a lunar module. Two astronauts would touch down on the moon while a third would remain with the service module in orbit around the moon. When the two astronauts finished their work on the surface, they'd blast off in the lunar module and rendezvous with the service module, and the three-man astronaut crew would journey back to Earth. This plan had promise because the LOR architecture required only one rocket, of a size that NASA could theoretically engineer, along with a smaller craft that could be designed with windows and controls specifically suited to making a lunar landing. The risk was that the astronauts would have no means of getting back to Earth if any of their rendezvous maneuvers ran aground. There was no margin for error.

After considerable debate, the engineers chose the LOR option in the summer of 1962, giving NASA a clear direction. Now all they had to do was build the entire Apollo system from scratch.

• • •

After his May 25 speech, Kennedy turned his attention to an upcoming summit with Soviet Premier Nikita Khrushchev in Austria. When Kennedy and Khrushchev sat down for lunch on June 3, the president congratulated the Soviet leader on the success of his manned space flight two months before with Gagarin. The conversation shifted to America's planned trip to the moon. When Khrushchev said he had concerns about the military aspects of such flights, Kennedy, testing the waters, suggested that the United States and Soviet Union go to the moon together.

John F. Kennedy and Premier Nikita Khrushchev at the Vienna summit on June 4, 1961.

Khrushchev wasn't interested. Asked about his conversation with Kennedy in Vienna by his son, Khrushchev admitted that, "If we cooperate, it will mean opening up our rocket program to them. We have only two hundred missiles, but they think we have many more." Khrushchev worried that Kennedy might launch a military strike if he knew how few missiles the Soviets actually had.

"So, when they say we have something to hide . . . ?" the Soviet leader was asked by his boy.

"It is just the opposite," he said. "We have nothing to hide. We have nothing. And we must hide it."

The rest of the Vienna summit didn't go well. Khrushchev was bossy and firm, especially with regard to the ongoing problems in Berlin, Germany. After World War II, Germany had been divided into two: West Germany, which was allied with the democratic Western nations, and East Germany, which was aligned with the communist Soviet Union. One huge inconvenience was that Berlin, the German capital, was located geographically in East Germany—but the West insisted on retaining control of half the city. Khrushchev wanted NATO forces to leave Berlin so the city could be united and under Soviet control. Kennedy didn't handle the discussion with Khrushchev particularly well, leaving the Soviet leader with the impression that the United States wouldn't act if West Berlin was cut off from the Western powers.

After the summit, stones and construction equipment were hastily moved to the makeshift border between East and West Berlin. Rather than building a better relationship with Western powers, it appeared the Soviets were going to build a wall.

chapter eighteen

Laying the Groundwork

President Kennedy knew how to use the media. He was the best communicator of his generation and one of the most telegenic men of his day, appearing natural and energetic on TV. The audience knew the events of his life—his family, his Ivy League education, his World War II heroism, his Catholic idealism—and the American people came to know him as charming, accomplished, and smart.

Starting on January 25, 1961, Kennedy began holding regular televised news conferences. Some of his supporters initially worried that he might make a mistake or bungle a policy idea, but Kennedy thought the unscripted openness was worth the risk. On live television, he learned to field questions like a shortstop, relying on his knowledge and intellect to figure out how to answer tough questions. The events were a bit like the televised broadcasts of manned space launches: The audience knew the time to tune in but not what would ultimately happen.

In these press conferences, Kennedy sometimes did make mistakes, but he also showed finesse and spontaneous wit under verbal fire. People could see his genuine feelings about issues. He knew to keep his answers short, concise, and on topic.

Television also proved to be well suited for use by space explorers. NASA committed to live broadcasts of future rockets launched at Cape Canaveral, allowing the American people to share the experience of space. For the three major American television networks at the time, NASA space events offered hours of drama and stunning visuals. NASA supplied the feeds from space for free, although covering blastoffs, touchdowns, and other aspects of programming remained expensive, leading the networks to form a pool and share some of their filmed footage. In addition to covering the live events, broadcasters also taped NASA launch rehearsals, giving them a supply of action footage to use as needed.

News coverage of space travel meant that over fifty million people could see their tax dollars at work. With each Mercury mission, the building blocks of America's Apollo moonshot snapped more firmly into place. Americans became stakeholders in the grand drama, partners in the adventure along with the astronauts and engineers. New Frontier America didn't hide its space activities until it had a confirmed success. Instead, it stood up before the camera and laid it all on the line.

A United States Marine helicopter lifts astronaut Virgil "Gus" Grissom from the Atlantic Ocean after his Liberty Bell 7 capsule lands, following a suborbital flight. President Kennedy would telephone Grissom aboard the USS *Randolph* to congratulate him on surviving the ordeal.

These broadcasts also went overseas, so America's accomplishments in space felt like they belonged to the world. This approach stood in stark contrast to the approach of the Soviet Union, where everything was kept secret, and even the Moscow phone book was classified.

In the summer of 1961, NASA was preparing for the second televised Mercury launch, which was scheduled for the third week of July. With the moonshot funding vote pending in Congress, NASA absolutely needed a successful mission. Astronaut Virgil Grissom was ready to board the Liberty Bell 7 for a fifteen-minute flight, which would be more sophisticated than Alan Shepard's earlier mission. Grissom had joined the Army Air Corps in World War II, earned a degree in mechanical engineering after the war, then reenlisted in the Air Force and flown one hundred low-flying combat missions in Korea without ever being hit. He was a natural pick for Project Mercury.

The launch went smoothly. Grissom soared to an altitude of 118 miles in 15 minutes and 37 seconds. Reentry went smoothly, but once the capsule splashed down in the Atlantic, a technical malfunction caused the side door to blow open, sending seawater gushing inside. Grissom watched as the capsule began to sink. Without waiting for the two Navy helicopters to retrieve him, Grissom scrambled out. When the choppers arrived, Grissom tried to attach a cable to the capsule, but water began entering his space suit through the collar. Just as he was beginning to sink, a helicopter hoisted him to safety.

Television viewers didn't see the drama unfold because the news stations aired the prerecorded "rehearsal" footage of the recovery rather than live footage. Viewers at home were confused because what they saw on their television screens was completely at odds with what they were hearing from the newscasters. Eventually the Navy recovery ship confirmed that Grissom was safe, and the use of the prerecorded footage was revealed—and widely criticized. By betraying their obligation to present the news truthfully, the television broadcasters had endangered public trust in their NASA programming.

"It won't happen again," promised the president of CBS News.

To get to the moon, NASA needed to create a master plan. Engineers began by identifying more than 10,000 separate tasks that had to be accomplished, each with a particular objective. By going carefully, one step at a time, progress would be made and the risk of error lowered. Many major corporations were hired by NASA to make component parts.

NASA divided the program into several phases. The one-man crews of Project Mercury had already proven that an astronaut could function in Earth's orbit and return alive. In the next phase, known as Project Gemini, two-man crews would perfect the techniques of joining and docking in space. In addition, Gemini would prove that humans could survive in space for up to two weeks, during which time astronauts would go outside the capsule for the very first space walks.

The Apollo phase would begin once data from the earlier missions was processed. Using three-man crews, Apollo would begin testing its orbiter and lander in Earth and lunar orbits. Only when all of these steps were perfected would an Apollo mission attempt to carry out the moon landing.

Two of the most pressing early tasks were choosing a site for the Apollo launchpad and choosing a location for NASA's new manned space project headquarters. Cape Canaveral had a number of benefits, but the problem was that NASA guidelines required a ten-mile buffer between the launch site and residential neighborhoods. To meet the requirement, NASA bought 80,000 acres of orchard land around the launch site, securing the location for future missions.

Back in 1958, Greenbelt, Maryland, had been chosen as the site of an early space flight center. But in choosing a flight center for manned space missions, Vice President Lyndon Johnson lobbied hard for Houston, in his home state of Texas. Other states also bid for the honor, including Massachusetts, Virginia, Missouri, Louisiana, and California, but after a number of backroom deals, NASA announced that Houston had won the bidding war. NASA's new Manned Spacecraft Center would function as the headquarters for the Apollo missions and future human spaceflight programs.

The decision transformed Houston, which soon became known as Space City, U.S.A. New businesses sprung up with names like Space City Bar-B-Q, Space Age Laminating Company, Astro Babysitters Agency, and the Apollo Restaurant, where the space burger on the menu was described as out of this world. Even Houston's new professional baseball and basketball teams got in on the action, naming themselves the Astros and the Rockets, which had orginated as a San Diego franchise.

Some people questioned the fairness of the Houston decision, but they didn't need to stay disappointed long. The space program had thousands more tasks to assign and contracts to sign. The work was just beginning, and companies and universities in multiple states were taking part.

chapter nineteen

Godspeed, John Glenn

Within sixteen days of the Liberty Bell 7 launch, President Kennedy once again had to congratulate Soviet Premier Nikita Khrushchev on another successful mission. While Grissom's launch had been a suborbital fifteen-minute flight, the Soviets countered by sending Vostok 2 up for an astonishing seventeen and a half trips around the Earth in a little over twenty-five hours.

During the Soviet flight, twenty-five-year-old cosmonaut Gherman Titov slept for thirty minutes, proving that people in space did not have to remain on high alert during the entire journey. They could relax, work, and sleep during their mission, suffering no more side effects than occasional motion sickness. The Soviets still hadn't fine-tuned their landing process, so Titov had to eject once his capsule reentered the Earth's atmosphere. He parachuted to a landing six hundred miles from Moscow, then was driven three miles to where his capsule had made a hard-impact landing.

NASA engineers were distraught. The Soviet mission had achieved goals they had set for their sixth Mercury mission, still four flights down the list. Once again, it seemed the chasm between the U.S. and Soviet space programs had grown.

Kennedy tried to downplay the importance of the Soviet mission, especially since tensions were also rising over the status of West Berlin. As many as two thousand East Germans—many of them well-educated and skilled—were crossing every day from Soviet-controlled East Germany to capitalist-democratic West Berlin. Instead of addressing the reasons East Germany's citizens were fleeing to the West, Khrushchev increased ground troops in the area and talked about Soviet nuclear superiority, trying to intimidate Kennedy and the Western powers and close the border to migration.

The president continued to seek cooperation as well as a nuclear test ban treaty with the Soviets, but he also made a show of American military preparations in West Germany. He issued a bland statement of "admiration" for Vostok 2, but he didn't say anything more. Behind the scenes, Kennedy told NASA to speed up the next Mercury launch.

The president stood by his commitment to keep West Berlin free and independent of East Germany. To stop the flow of its citizens to the West, on August 13, 1962, East Germany erected an eighty-seven-mile barbed-wire fence dividing communist

East Berlin from democratic West Berlin. The wall went up without warning, and in the weeks that followed it was reinforced with concrete barriers and guard towers.

The wall outraged Kennedy as an affront to human decency, but he didn't overreact. Within a few weeks, the crisis cooled. "It's not a very nice solution," Kennedy said, "but the wall is a hell of a lot better than a war."

NASA engineers worked double time to reach the moon. Some engineers worried that speeding up the research could result in disaster, but the Soviets had forced Kennedy's hand. Fears of a hammer-and-sickle Soviet flag planted on the moon left the administration with few options other than work at breakneck speed and innovate new technology.

One option for the United States was the U.S. Air Force's Atlas rocket. It had five times the thrust of earlier rockets, and it was considered ready to go, although it had experienced several explosions during unmanned testing. Wernher von Braun's Saturn design was still years away from being ready for launch. In September, NASA sent up an unmanned Mercury capsule using an Atlas rocket, and the mission came off without a hitch.

Kennedy worried that momentum for the moonshot was fading. The press corps began to focus on stories critical of the space program. For example, Dr. Al Hibbs, chief of space sciences at the Jet Propulsion Laboratory in Pasadena, said that the United States had "less than a 50-50 chance" of beating the

Soviets to the moon. Other experts doubted if the United States would ever be able to catch up to the Soviets. This was not the kind of news Kennedy wanted to read.

Like many Americans, President Kennedy started 1962 concerned about the space race. He had to say something about it in his State of the Union Address—after all, he had made the promise of the moonshot only seven months before—but this time his remarks were considerably less confident, acknowledging that the United States might not win: "This nation belongs among the first to explore [the moon]. And among the first, if not the first, we shall be." He was trying to lower the country's expectations and assure them that it was all right if the United States lost the race. Regardless of the Soviets, NASA was going to the moon—because first or not, the moonshot was worthwhile.

A month later, the nation focused on Friendship 7 and astronaut John Glenn's mission to orbit the Earth. Forty-year-old Glenn—the oldest of the Mercury Seven—had a wide, boyish face, a bright smile, and a positive attitude, which made him impossible not to like. He had been chosen to man America's first full orbital flight.

Friendship 7 was an airtight, watertight, soundproof marvel of engineering, containing seven miles of wiring and insulated shields designed to protect its pilot from both 3,000-degree heat and cold more numbing than the Arctic. The instrument panel had more than a hundred dials and switches. On

February 20, 1962, Glenn woke up for his fourteenth scheduled attempt at launch. The earlier dates had all been canceled due to technical concerns or uncooperative weather. This time it was all clear. At 9:47 a.m., the Atlas rocket fired and lifted off. The capsule communicator for the mission said, "Godspeed, John Glenn."

More than forty million American homes tuned in to watch as Glenn soared skyward. But there were problems: Late in the mission, an autopilot malfunction forced him to fly portions of his final orbits manually. Then a signal during reentry indicated that Friendship 7's heat shield was probably loose. If it came off, Glenn would not survive reentry.

Moments later, Glenn lost radio contact for four and a half minutes, amplifying the distance between Glenn and the world. When radio contact was restored, NASA engineers let out a collective sigh of relief. Glenn orbited Earth three times in just under five hours at a speed of 17,545 miles per hour and an altitude of 160 miles. The trip back to Earth was a bumpy ride, but the capsule splashed down safely in the Atlantic.

Pride in the space program reignited, and people talked about the moonshot again. Astronauts Alan Shepard and Deke Slayton summed up the post–Friendship 7 excitement best: "The distance to the moon was starting to lessen."

Though Glenn's three orbits were much less impressive than Gherman Titov's seventeen laps, NASA seemed to be gaining ground on the Soviets. On February 23, Kennedy presented Glenn with the NASA Distinguished Service Metal.

• • •

That spring, Friendship 7 went on a second mission: a thirty-city "Around the World with Friendship 7" tour to promote U.S. space achievements. Loaded onto a giant cargo plane, the capsule was displayed in London, Sri Lanka, Mexico, Nigeria, Tokyo, and Bombay (now Mumbai), among other places. The international tour was an ideal advertisement for Kennedy's New Frontier, but more than that, it was a science education program that ultimately benefited people around the world.

National hero John Glenn visited the Seattle World's Fair on May 10. While there, he spoke to members of the 100,000 Foot Club, a group of test pilots who had attained that altitude in balloons, rockets, and other aircraft. Glenn got all the attention at the event, but no one knew at the time that another man on the stage would soon eclipse even Glenn's fame: His name was Neil Armstrong.

chapter twenty

Peace in Space

While John Glenn's three orbits aboard Friendship 7 rekindled the nation's giddy New Frontier optimism about space, relations with the Soviet Union remained tense. Every day, people in East Germany risked their lives to escape to the West Germany sector of Berlin. The fear of nuclear war was widespread. Both the United States and the Soviet Union pressed ahead with plans to develop intercontinental ballistic missiles and spy systems that could be considered "weaponizing space."

Hoping to negotiate an agreement that would prevent further militarization of space, Kennedy wrote a three-page letter to Soviet Premier Nikita Khrushchev on March 7, 1962, suggesting that the two superpowers "could render no greater service to mankind through our space programs than by the joint establishment of an early operational weather satellite system." He suggested exchanging space-related equipment, scientific data, and astronauts. He offered the possibility of future missions to Mars or Venus, although he did not offer to share the Apollo moonshot.

Kennedy mentioned NASA's steady technological progress, knowing that the Kremlin hated such transparency. The U.S. government's message was clear: Kennedy's New Frontier stood for freedom and openness, while the Kremlin was all about secrecy and hidden totalitarian agendas. Kennedy made his letter to the Soviet leader public, eager to let the world know that the United States thought of space in peaceful terms.

Khrushchev was afraid of being tricked by Kennedy. Behind the scenes, the Soviets had already weaponized space, having begun high-altitude testing of nuclear bombs during the latter half of 1961. This was part of a nuclear testing program that had resulted in 2,014 detonations between 1949 and 1962.

The United States wasn't innocent of such testing, either. Throughout the 1950s and early 1960s the federal government regularly tested nuclear weapons in the upper atmosphere.

Kennedy said he wanted a ban on nuclear testing in the atmosphere and in outer space, but he didn't want to fall behind if the Soviets were already developing a nuclear space program. Despite Kennedy's desire to keep the space race from becoming an arms race, the military and the CIA authorized a number of space-based weapons programs.

To protect the United States from nuclear attack, in December 1961 a private contractor had begun working on an antiballistic-missile defense system. A few weeks later, Kennedy changed his mind and pulled funding for the program, deciding that it was wiser to find a peaceful solution than to try to build a multibillion-dollar cocoon over America. (The idea returned in the 1980s when President Ronald Reagan proposed a similar program nicknamed "Star Wars," which cost $30 billion before it was abandoned due to technical problems, expense, and concerns that it complicated arms control discussions with the Soviets.) Today the U.S. government does have an impressive array of missile defense programs to help protect the American homeland.

When the Soviets refused to sign an agreement banning nuclear tests in space, Kennedy reluctantly approved a series of additional atmospheric nuclear tests. The president sent an advisor to deliver a speech at a meeting of defense industry and government officials discussing aerospace technology. The speech began by restating Kennedy's fervent support of using space for peaceful purposes, then it changed direction. Speaking for the president, Kennedy's advisor said that the United States should prepare to use space both offensively and defensively, if necessary.

Kennedy used the speech to deliver a message to Khrushchev: The U.S. military was ready to meet any and all Soviet threats—even, if necessary, in outer space.

• • •

Mercury astronaut Scott Carpenter of Colorado dressed for spaceflight. He was a U.S. Naval officer and aviator. On May 24, 1962, Carpenter flew into space atop the Mercury-Atlas 7 rocket, becoming the second American (after John Glenn) to orbit the Earth.

By the end of May 1962, NASA was preparing for its next launch, which would be similar to the Glenn mission but include additional scientific experiments. The astronaut chosen for the mission was Scott Carpenter, a longtime Navy test pilot from Colorado who had a reputation for staying calm in tense situations.

The mission was a success, but Carpenter made several mistakes in preparation for reentry into the atmosphere. Due to these mistakes, his capsule overshot the planned splashdown point by 250 miles. Carpenter had to escape the spacecraft before it sank, scrambling into an inflatable raft. He was out of radio contact for thirty-nine minutes, while the ocean tossed him around. After three hours at sea, he was finally rescued.

NASA officials were embarrassed by the breakdown in procedure. As had become traditional with the Mercury astronauts, Kennedy invited Carpenter and his family to the White House on June 5 but didn't extend the warmth and red-carpet fanfare that had welcomed the previous astronauts. Beyond being a commentary on Carpenter's errors, the president's distance may have stemmed from preoccupation over another concern in space: Twenty-four hours earlier, the United States had launched a rocket equipped with a nuclear bomb set to explode at an altitude of thirty miles. During the first attempted launch on June 2, radar lost track of the missile, so the mission had to be stopped. The rocket fell harmlessly into the Pacific. But the failed mission revealed to the Soviet Union that the United

States was doing its own high-altitude nuclear testing.

Kennedy's hope for a test ban agreement with the Soviets was lost. Instead, the United States continued to test its own rockets and nuclear weapons. On July 9, 1962, it detonated a warhead at a record altitude of nearly 250 miles, well into outer space. The power was so great that the enormous fireball could be seen flashing as far away as Honolulu. It was by far the largest nuclear weapon detonated to date, a hundred times more powerful than the bomb dropped on Hiroshima in World War II.

There were also some peaceful developments in space in the summer of 1962. In August, NASA's Mariner 2 probe headed for Venus on a three-and-half-month scientific mission to measure planetary temperatures and the magnetic fields and charged particle environments between planets. In addition, the United States made the first direct television connection between continents with the launch of Telstar 1, a satellite owned by a private telecommunications company that successfully transmitted signals between the United States and Europe. What made this mission different from those that came before was that most of the funding for the satellite came from industry, not NASA or the military.

In the summer of 1962, Republican senator Barry Goldwater of Arizona gave a major speech about space, promoting its military use. "How can we guarantee that space will be used for peaceful purposes without having the means to defend such a doctrine?" he asked the National Association of Rocketry on

President Kennedy tours NASA facilities in Huntsville, Alabama. The U.S. government developed ballistic rockets under the guidance of Wernher von Braun called Redstone, Jupiter-C, Juno, and the Saturn 1B at the Marshall Space Flight Center there.

July 17. "It is our view that international law or agreement cannot exist without the physical means to enforce it."

Goldwater, who was already being mentioned as a possible 1964 Republican presidential candidate, accused the Kennedy administration of "gambling with national survival" by making military objectives in space secondary to peaceful scientific accomplishments. In August, Goldwater and his fellow Republicans in the Senate opened a debate on the subject of space militarization.

Kennedy knew Goldwater was looking for a calculated issue like the "missile gap" argument he himself had used against Eisenhower and Nixon. The White House argued that spending on the military space program had doubled in one year, to $1.5 billion, but for security reasons it couldn't share details publicly—and the Republicans knew it.

On September 11, Kennedy toured the space facility at Huntsville, Alabama, inspecting a Saturn I rocket and other technology aimed at powering NASA astronauts to the moon. Rocket scientist Wernher von Braun showed the president a drawing of a Saturn rocket, saying, "This is the vehicle designed to fulfill your promises to put a man on the moon in this decade."

Karl Heimburg, Huntsville's test lab director, told the president that the booster produced 1.3 million pounds of thrust, outperforming anything the Soviets had. When the rocket's engines were ignited for testing, Kennedy's jaw dropped.

Next, Kennedy visited the NASA Launch Operations

Center on Cape Canaveral, one of the world's most sophisticated high-technology government facilities. Kennedy thrilled at all he saw during his two-and-a-half-hour tour. Beaming with confidence, he gave a brief pep rally speech, saying, "We shall be first!" The Apollo moonshot was becoming more real with each passing day.

Part IV

PROJECTS GEMINI AND APOLLO

chapter twenty-one

Not Because It Is Easy

A s part of his space tour in September 1962, President Kennedy left Cape Canaveral and headed to Houston. Thousands of people turned out to greet him on his arrival. "I do not know whether the people of the Southwest realize the profound effect the whole space program will have on the economy of this section of the country," he said to the crowd. "The scientists, engineers, and technical people who will be attracted here really make the Southwest a great center of scientific and industrial research as this nation reaches out to the moon."

On September 12, Kennedy went to the football stadium at Houston's Rice University, where 30,000 people waited for him to speak about going to the moon. The weather was blazing hot and humid, even at 10:00 a.m. Knowing that his moonshot speech to Congress the previous year had been a bit tame,

President John F. Kennedy spoke before a huge crowd at Rice University's football stadium on September 12, 1962, in Houston, Texas, on the nation's space effort.

Kennedy decided to fill the stadium with a soaring, inspiring speech.

The president of Rice University introduced Kennedy to the roaring crowd, and committed the university to developing graduate-level programs in space science and other specific topics that would help America meet its Space Age needs.

When Kennedy took the stage, the crowd went wild. Speaking with poise and grace, the president positioned science and technological research at the forefront of American life. His speech reflected on 50,000 years of history, from cavemen to jet pilots to astronauts. "Surely the opening vistas of space promise high costs and hardships, as well as high reward," he said. "So it is not surprising that some would have us stay where we are a little longer to rest, to wait. But this city of Houston, this state of Texas, this country of the United States, were not built by those who waited and rested and wished to look behind them. This country was conquered by those who moved forward—and so will space."

The president insisted that the United States—no matter what the financial cost—had to dominate space. "The exploration of space," he said, "will go ahead whether we join in it or not, and it is one of the great adventures of all time. . . . Those who came before us made certain that this country rode the first waves of the industrial revolution, the first waves of modern invention, and the first waves of nuclear power. And this generation does not intend to founder in the backwash of the coming age of space. We mean to be part of it. We mean to lead it."

The heart of the speech connected NASA to America's frontier tradition and the concept of American exceptionalism. Space represented the grand historic challenge of an unexplored frontier for new generations of trailblazers. "We choose to go to the moon in this decade and do the other things, not because they are easy, but because they are hard, because that goal will serve to organize and measure the best of our energies and skills, because that challenge is one that we are willing to accept, one we are unwilling to postpone, and one which we intend to win."

When Kennedy finished his remarks, the audience erupted in ecstatic applause.

As the president exited the stage, he nodded at the nearby

President John F. Kennedy emerging from inside a model of the futuristic Apollo capsule during his tour of NASA's new Manned Spacecraft Center in Houston, Texas.

NASA administrators with a wide grin. "All right," he said. "Now you guys do the details!"

Thousands of people stood along the road as Kennedy drove to the temporary Manned Spacecraft Center's Research Division, one of twelve Houston-area NASA sites. He stayed there twice as long as scheduled. At one point he climbed into the cockpit of an Apollo Command Module mock-up, which had been designed to test the crew seats and instrument panels.

In part, the speech and remarks he made that day were responses to his Republican critics. He held up the moonshot as evidence of human achievement, a slap at Barry Goldwater's argument that NASA was a distraction from the allegedly more important military uses of space.

Kennedy also had to be careful in how he spoke about the Eisenhower administration. A few weeks before, former president Eisenhower had published an article in the *Saturday Evening Post* criticizing Kennedy's expensive NASA expansion. "By all means, we must carry on our explorations in space, but I frankly do not see the need for continuing this effort as such a fantastically expensive crash program," the former president wrote. "From here on, I think we should proceed in an orderly, scientific way, building one accomplishment on another, rather than engaging in a mad effort to win a stunt race."

Kennedy didn't want to turn the space program into a hotly debated political issue. In 1962, it was still seen as a uniting, bipartisan national endeavor. The president didn't want

Republicans in the midterm elections to begin saying, "Why the great hurry to get to the moon?"

In an effort not to trigger a fierce debate over the issue or further anger the former president, Kennedy resisted the temptation to respond. Instead, he finished his tour by visiting a private aircraft factory in St. Louis, Missouri, where the Gemini two-man space capsule was being built. There, Kennedy inspected a Gemini capsule mock-up and met with top company executives, highlighting how the space program supported the New Frontier economy, resulting in growth in private businesses. Aware that Congress was showing signs of pushing back against NASA's growing budget, Kennedy wanted to remind taxpayers of how their money was being spent. He believed public funding of the moonshot was a down payment on the future greatness of the United States.

While Kennedy was away on his space tour, new trouble erupted in Cuba. Since the Bay of Pigs disaster the previous year, the United States had continued to try to knock Fidel Castro out of power. It had tried assassination plots, attempted to undermine the Cuban economy, and created plans to block the island nation's naval ports. Worried that the United States was going to invade his country and in desperate need of a strong ally, Castro agreed to allow the Soviet Union to install intermediate-range nuclear missiles in Cuba.

In response, Kennedy asked Congress for authority to order 150,000 reserve soldiers to active duty for a year. The Soviet

Union considered this an act of aggression and said it would stand with Cuba in case of war.

Kennedy didn't want a war, but he wouldn't allow the United States to be bullied. At a press conference on September 13, he addressed the situation directly. "Let me make this clear," he said. "If at any time the Communist buildup in Cuba were to endanger or interfere with our security in any way, including our base at Guantánamo, our passage to the Panama Canal, our missile and space activities at Cape Canaveral, or the lives of American citizens in the country . . . then this country will do whatever must be done."

chapter twenty-two

Winning at Any Cost

While Kennedy was touring America's space facilities, thirty-one Project Gemini finalists were waiting nervously to see who would make the final cut and become astronauts. Nine slots were available—two more than for Mercury—since Gemini's launch schedule would be more compressed. This time, NASA didn't look for test pilots; they wanted intellectual giants to help solve the complex problems of space.

On September 14, 1962, nine men received phone calls from one of the current Mercury Seven astronauts. Neil Armstrong got a call from Deke Slayton. When asked if he still wanted to be an astronaut, Armstrong said, "Yes, sir."

The astronauts were told there would be eleven or twelve manned Gemini flights, and that one of the nine of them would be the first man on the moon.

Group portrait of the second group of men selected to be astronauts in NASA's Project Gemini space program, 1963. Bottom row left to right: James Lovell, Jim McDivitt, and Pete Conrad (1930–99); second row: Elliot See (1927–66) and Thomas Stafford; third row: Edward White (1930–67) and John Young (1930–2018); fourth row: Neil Armstrong (1930–2012) and Frank Borman.

Three days later, the "Gemini Nine" were introduced to the public. The crowd cheered when their names were read: civilian pilots Neil Armstrong and Elliot M. See Jr.; Air Force officers Frank Borman, James McDivitt, Thomas Stafford, and Edward White; and Naval aviators Charles "Pete" Conrad, James A. Lovell, and John W. Young. Some in the press called them the "New Nine" or the "Kennedy Moon Corps."

Introducing the new astronauts was a way to keep public enthusiasm high as Congress began debating the increases in NASA's budget. Costs were rising. By September, Gemini's projected cost had risen from $530 million to $745 million ($6.2 billion in today's dollars) due to the need to reconfigure and develop new systems.

President Kennedy had inspired Americans to reach for the moon, but it soon became clear the message was really targeted only at men. When women tried to apply to America's astronaut corps, they were turned away. For example, when Susan Marie Scott of Kentucky asked to apply to Project Gemini, she received a response from O.B. Lloyd Jr., director of NASA's Office of Public Services and Information, who wrote, "Many women are employed in the program—some of them are in extremely important scientific posts. But we have no present plans to employ women in space flights. There are no women pilots to our knowledge, who have the degrees of scientific and flight training required for the success of those missions. Since there is no shortage of qualified male candidates, there is no need to train women for space flight at this stage in the program."

NASA didn't specifically say that applicants had to be male, but decades of discrimination in the military resulted in the unfair assumption that women were simply unqualified for the jobs. The military banned women from flying high-performance aircraft, and civilian companies rarely hired female pilots.

One advocate for women in space was Dr. Randolph Lovelace, an aeromedicine pioneer only loosely affiliated with NASA. He believed that women would actually make better astronauts, physically: On average, they were shorter and smaller, needed less food and oxygen, and had better blood circulation and fewer heart problems. Using private funds, he began testing nineteen women. Thirteen of them passed the same tests as the original Mercury Seven astronauts, and many tested better than most of the Gemini Nine. Unofficially named the "Mercury Thirteen," these female pilots ranged in age from twenty-three to forty-one. They were flight instructors, homemakers, scientists, and Korean War contributors.

When NASA director James Webb learned about the Mercury Thirteen, he was unimpressed. He believed that all of NASA's astronaut-training energy had to be targeted toward the moonshot, rather than a project focused on getting women into space. In other words, it wasn't the time for a shift in gender. That didn't stop the American press from lionizing these women's test results. Some of the choice headlines read:

"Astrogals Can't Wait for Space," "Spunky Mom Eyes Heavens," and "Why Not 'Astronauttes' Also?"

The women pushed for a meeting at the special subcommittee of the House Committee on Science and Astronautics. Several female pilots spoke about women's equality, but they were overshadowed by John Glenn, who argued that funding women in space drained money needed for the moonshot. The committee voted with Glenn and against the women.

The following year, the Soviet Union did what the Americans wouldn't and launched the first woman into space. Aboard the Vostok 6, cosmonaut Valentina Tereshkova became a global hero by making forty-eight Earth orbits over the course of seventy hours.

Lovelace continued to advocate for female astronauts, but in December 1965, he and his wife were killed in a plane crash. Almost twenty years would pass before Sally Ride became the first American women in space, serving as mission specialist on space shuttle flight of June 18–29, 1983. While American women weren't allowed to be astronauts in the 1950s, 1960s, and 1970s, many held essential jobs at NASA, working behind the scenes. Katherine Johnson, an African American mathematician, calculated rocket trajectories for NASA's Project Mercury. In 2016, her amazing life story was told in the movie *Hidden Figures*. Computer scientist and engineer Margaret Hamilton, working out of the Massachusetts Institute of Technology laboratory, innovated the onboard flight guidance software that allowed Neil Armstrong and Buzz Aldrin to land safely on the moon.

• • •

Astronaut Wally Schirra became America's next space hero when he took off on October 3, 1962, aboard the Mercury-Atlas 8. He named his spacecraft Sigma 7—"Sigma" for the Greek symbol often used in mathematics to represent the sum of the elements in an equation, and "7" for the Mercury Seven. "Not a fancy name like Freedom or Faith," Schirra later said. "Not that I didn't appreciate those names, but I wanted to prove that it was a team of people working together to make this vehicle go."

During his nine-hour flight, Schirra smoothly conducted a series of tests. His mission focused on engineering: the performance and operation of the spacecraft, the tracking and communication systems, and the effects of prolonged weightlessness on the astronaut himself. While NASA was proud that the mission went off flawlessly, their excitement was tempered by the knowledge that two months earlier the Soviet Union had smashed the record for human endurance in space when cosmonaut Andriyan Nikolayev piloted Vostok 3 through sixty-four Earth orbits over the course of almost four days. While the United States could be proud of its achievements, the perceived gap in the space race was not closing.

Almost two weeks after splashdown, Schirra and his family visited with President Kennedy in the Oval Office. Since the president seemed friendly and at ease, the astronaut and his family did not realize that Kennedy had just heard troubling news.

Twenty-five minutes before the Schirras arrived, Kennedy was told that surveillance photos of Cuba confirmed the construction of launch bases for Soviet nuclear missiles. Though not yet operational, these bases posed an enormous threat, putting Soviet nuclear missiles just one hundred miles from American soil.

When the astronaut and his family left the White House, Kennedy immediately called in his senior advisors and reviewed the top secret U-2 photos of Cuba, which showed fourteen canvas-covered missile trailers. The team considered possible responses, including air strikes, invasion, and naval blockades. But Kennedy worried that any military response could trigger war.

On October 18, Kennedy learned that two medium-range ballistic missile sites in Cuba could be operational within weeks. On October 22, the president faced the nation in a televised address. He stated that the United States would never tolerate Soviet offensive weapons in the Caribbean. In response, the military would enforce a naval blockade to prevent Soviet ships from moving missiles into Cuba.

The nation feared an all-out nuclear war with the Soviets. Finally, on October 28, after thirteen nerve-racking days and a complex series of communications, Kennedy and Soviet leader Khrushchev agreed to a peaceful resolution to what became known as the Cuban Missile Crisis. The Soviets agreed to remove the missile bases from Cuba, and Kennedy promised that the U.S. wouldn't invade the island nation. In addition,

A gaggle of customers in a California appliance store gather in the electronics department on October 27, 1962, to watch President John F. Kennedy deliver a televised address to the nation on the subject of the Cuban Missile Crisis.

Kennedy secretly committed to removing American Jupiter missiles from Turkey within a year.

The close call changed both Kennedy and Khrushchev. The experience of living with their fingers on the nuclear button for thirteen days caused the two leaders to open a hotline between Moscow and Washington and to begin a correspondence aimed at lowering global tensions. They also began serious negotiations for what became the Limited Nuclear Test Ban Treaty, signed the following August to limit atmospheric and underwater nuclear tests.

President Kennedy's ambitious space program began as his way of putting the country on a grand mission of renewal. The Korean War and the prolonged Cold War had aged the country, and he believed the space program would offer the United States new energy, originality, optimism, and a sense of both individual achievement and teamwork.

But after the Cuban Missile Crisis, Kennedy began questioning the moonshot and the reasoning behind the space race. With total annual spending that had grown from $500 million to billions in two years, he faced growing resistance to the program's cost. The days of blank checks were coming to an end. NASA found that the spending on manned space missions was draining funds from work on communication satellites, Mars probes, meteorite studies, and other unmanned missions.

Some within NASA wanted to concentrate all the money on the moonshot. Others wanted to fund other space missions as well. The debate took a new turn on November 13, 1962, when Kennedy received a report indicating that there was no real space race with the Soviets. For all the Sputniks and Vostoks, there was no evidence that the Soviets were building facilities and equipment capable of sending a cosmonaut to the moon. Khrushchev's space efforts were geared toward building a space station, not taking a moon walk.

If the report was true, then the United States was racing against itself to get to the moon. This encouraged the position of maintaining funding for a broad space program, rather than going with the moon-only argument. If there were budget cuts to be made, they should be applied at least in part to the moon mission.

On November 21, 1962, Kennedy called his space advisors to the White House for a talk about space priorities and the role of the moonshot. In the meeting, Kennedy asked NASA director James Webb if he thought the moon mission was the agency's top priority program. "I think it is one of the top-priority programs," Webb said.

Kennedy disagreed. "I think it is the top priority," he said, noting that some other programs could slip back six or nine months without consequences. Although Kennedy had seen the U-2 reconnaissance photos discounting the possibility of a Soviet moonshot, he was still worried the Soviets would beat the United States. He also knew that if word leaked that the Soviets weren't actually racing America to the moon, congressional funding for Project Apollo would dry up. "Everything that we do ought to really be tied into getting onto the Moon ahead of the Russians," he said.

The importance of reaching the moon had everything to do with recent events and the Cuban Missile Crisis. At the end of the meeting about space, Webb said, "I have some feeling that you might not have been as successful on Cuba if we hadn't flown John Glenn and demonstrated we had a real overall technical capability here."

Kennedy wasn't just arguing for the Apollo program. He was arguing for a new era in which technological superiority was power. The moonshot was a showcase for America's scientific and technological might. It was inspirational, but it was more than that. While NASA's eventual moon mission was peaceful, the rocketry being developed was also a weapon in the Cold War struggle.

chapter twenty-three

Staying Moonbound

ASA closed out 1962 with a success as its unmanned Mariner 2 probe became the first space vehicle to make meaningful contact with Venus—yet another space objective toward which both the United States and the Soviet Union had been striving. In February 1961, the Soviets had launched the first Venus probe, Venera 1, but it missed the mark by 62,000 miles due to a communication error. A year later, they tried again, but that spacecraft failed to escape Earth's orbit.

On December 14, 1962, the United States did it. After 110 days in space, Mariner 2 arrived, sending back valuable information about the planet. Scientists had speculated that Venus had an environment that might support life. What they found were blisteringly high temperatures and crushing atmospheric pressure.

The Mariner 2 mission marked another turning point, giving scientists a firsthand look at both space and one of our neighboring planets. It was a win for the purely scientific side of space exploration, and it put the United States firmly ahead of the Soviets in the race to explore the solar system.

Kennedy promoted the success of Mariner 2 to encourage greater congressional funding for NASA's manned space program. The president's proposed federal budget for 1964 included $5.7 billion in spending on space, a 75 percent increase from the previous year. This was an astounding amount of money, more than 3.5 percent of total national spending.

Being number one in space was expensive, Kennedy said. Conservative Republicans set out to block the increase. Former President Eisenhower said, "Anybody who would spend $40 billion in a race to the moon for national prestige is nuts."

Critics also worried about how the money was being spent. NASA's staff had nearly doubled in one year. Space technology centers were being developed in states across the South, and some considered this nothing more than a way to keep the Southern states voting for Democrats.

Kennedy believed the space program was important because it showed the world what America could accomplish. In only two years as president, having given NASA the funding it needed, Kennedy had taken the country from launching its first Mercury astronauts to exploring Venus and revolutionizing space technology. Computer science programs were becoming widespread in colleges and universities. Educational opportunities in the sciences were soaring. NASA's high-profile advances were a constant reminder of what was possible in fields like astronomy, aerospace, and physics.

In April 1963, under pressure to cut $700 million from the Apollo program, Kennedy asked Vice President Lyndon Johnson to conduct a review of NASA expenses and programs. Kennedy and Johnson disagreed about a lot of issues, but they both supported the moonshot goal.

Johnson had a keen knowledge of politics. He urged Kennedy to argue that "our space program has an overriding urgency that cannot be calculated solely in terms of industrial, scientific, or military development." If lawmakers criticized NASA, Johnson said to call them soft on communism. Johnson warned that if the NASA budget were to be reduced, the "future of society is at stake." The vice president prepared a report showing that the manned space program was a pressing national security issue. He laid out how a moon landing would result in long-term benefits in international prestige, scientific breakthroughs, and economic windfalls.

Nothing generated the same level of excitement as an actual journey to space. On May 15, NASA once again showed taxpayers their money in action when astronaut Gordon Cooper took off aboard Faith 7 for the sixth and final Project Mercury launch. While some Americans had started to lose interest in the semi-regular launches and splashdowns, Cooper's flight was different because it lasted more than thirty-four hours.

Cooper was known for his in-flight calmness, which was tested when problems developed in the stabilization and flight control systems. Instead of relying on autopilot for reentry, Cooper had to fly the old-fashioned way. As carbon-dioxide levels climbed dangerously inside the cabin, Cooper managed to control the spacecraft manually, using his view through the capsule's window to properly orient the craft for reentry. Despite the problems, Cooper splashed down with amazing accuracy, landing just four and a half miles from the recovery ship.

A week later, Major Cooper met with Kennedy at the White House to receive the NASA Distinguished Service Medal. Kennedy used the opportunity to remind people of the importance of manned space missions. "One of the things which warmed us the most during this flight," the president said, "was the realization that however extraordinary computers may be, that we are still ahead of them and that man is still the most extraordinary computer of all. His judgment, his nerve, and the lessons he can learn from experience still make him unique and, therefore, make manned flight necessary."

Despite this and other successes of the space program, in early summer the Senate Republican Policy Committee questioned the costs of the Gemini and Apollo programs, asking if a trip to the moon was more important than education, healthcare, and other challenges closer to home. The House Committee on Science and Aeronautics combed through NASA's projects and identified $490 million in cuts. Some suggested a slowdown in the program to save money. NASA administrator James Webb warned that cuts of more than $400 million would interfere with the effort to land an American on the moon within the decade.

Some in Congress criticized the space program because it focused on scientific exploration, while the Soviet program was almost certainly oriented toward national defense. They may have had a point, because it was becoming unclear whether the Soviets were aiming for the moon at all. Wernher von Braun regularly argued that the Soviets were winning the space race, an idea also promoted by Soviet Premier Nikita Khrushchev for his own purposes. But in fact, no one in the U.S. government really knew what the Soviets were up to. A CIA report in December 1962 indicated that there was no firm evidence the Soviets were working on a moonshot of their own, but it couldn't rule out that such a program existed. If this report was made public, it would have undermined the argument that the moon-shot was the ultimate trophy in the global struggle between democracy and communism. In this regard, the only thing NASA officials feared more than a strong Soviet moon program was a weak one. If the Soviets were to admit they were behind the United States, NASA's funding would be slashed.

In early 1963, the Soviets were experiencing setbacks in trying to send an unmanned vehicle to the moon, with three unsuccessful missions in the first four months of the year. The first failed to escape Earth's orbit, the second couldn't find its orbit of the moon, and the last missed the moon altogether. The

Soviets also launched a probe to Mars, but it disappeared into space due to an antenna malfunction. These expensive failures reduced Soviet enthusiasm for the moon. If there was a moon race at all, it seemed that the United States was the clear front-runner.

The State Department was becoming anxious about the lack of progress toward developing nuclear treaties and agreements with the Soviet Union. The United States government wanted to ban nuclear weapons in space, and feared the Soviets were stalling negotiations until they had a nuclear bomb in orbit. On June 10, 1963, Kennedy delivered a speech at American University announcing that later that summer the United States, Great Britain, and the Soviet Union would begin three-way talks aimed at banning atmospheric and underwater nuclear tests.

"The United States, as the world knows, will never start a war," Kennedy said. "We do not want a war. We do not now expect a war. This generation of Americans has already had enough—more than enough—of war and hate and oppression. We shall be prepared if others wish it. We shall be alert to try to stop it. But we shall also do our part to build a world of peace where the weak are safe and the strong are just."

Khrushchev told his aides that Kennedy's speech was "the best speech by any president since Roosevelt."

Not long after the address, Kennedy traveled to West Germany for meetings with the chancellor Konrad Adenauer. On

On June 26, 1963, President Kennedy speaks before the Brandenburg Gate in Berlin, telling the enthusiastic crowd in this divided German city, "Ich bin ein Berliner" (translation: I am a Berliner).

June 26, Kennedy delivered a speech to 450,000 people crowded into a plaza in West Berlin. In his remarks, the president advocated "the right to be free" over "the failures of the Communist system."

In fewer than seven hundred words, Kennedy offered hope to those on the other side of the wall, declaring, "Freedom is indivisible, and when one man is enslaved, all are not free." The speech lifted the morale of the city. It also showed the Soviet Union that despite the president's call for peace, the battle for hearts and minds around the world would remain fierce.

chapter twenty-four

Astronauts and Cosmonauts Together

The battle over the budget for space continued into 1963. Former president Dwight Eisenhower said that "a spectacular dash to the moon" would deepen America's debt and be an ongoing burden for taxpayers. Civil rights leaders pointed to the need for fighting urban poverty and disease at home instead of funding a moonshot. Even scientists questioned the value of manned space travel, arguing that unmanned probes were cheaper than manned missions.

President Kennedy held fast. "The point of the matter always has been not only of our excitement or interest in being on the moon," he said, "but the capacity to dominate space, which would be demonstrated by moon flight." The president considered the space program essential to the United States' identity as a leading free world power.

In the Soviet Union, Premier Nikita Khrushchev faced budget problems of his own. Competing with the United States in space was a backbreaking expense for the Soviets, who had experienced a number of embarrassing, high-profile space failures in recent years. Hunting for a way out of the space race, the Kremlin began sending out feelers to see whether America might be interested in a joint U.S.-Soviet moon mission.

Although Kennedy and Khrushchev had casually discussed a joint mission in 1961, this more serious proposal came as a surprise. Most U.S. government officials who heard the idea dismissed it for both strategic and political reasons. Some thought the Soviets were trying to damage Kennedy's 1964 reelection effort.

Kennedy was more open to the idea. He weighed the benefits of using the moonshot to win the Cold War against the potentially greater value of using it to build world peace. If ending the Cold War and improving global relations required partnering with the Soviets in space, Kennedy was interested.

The president had been focused on the issue of war and peace since he had attended an eighteen-minute attack simulation exercise sponsored by the military in Colorado. Kennedy watched a simulated Russian nuclear strike on the United States, seeing intercontinental missiles flattening American cities. The president was haunted by the idea that if such a devastating attack were to occur, the United States would have no choice but to launch its own missiles, possibly destroying life on Earth.

Faced with this doomsday possibility, the idea of giving up a little national prestige to achieve peace with the Soviets seemed sensible. A joint effort to the moon would also save massive amounts of money for both superpowers, and it would give NASA access to the details of the Soviet space program.

But Kennedy knew the risks were enormous. Any suggestion of working with the Soviets would invite attacks from people claiming the United States was falling into a trap. Sharing information from NASA with the Soviets could risk exposing satellite secrets, private business innovations, and classified intelligence. It could also put military programs at risk. On a practical level, the countries had different engineering approaches and technologies that would be difficult to merge.

Still, the lure of peace was hard to resist. Having so recently faced the real possibility of nuclear war during the Cuban Missile Crisis, Kennedy wasn't going to dismiss the idea without giving it thorough consideration.

Change was in the air in the summer of 1963. On August 28, a coalition of Civil Rights groups staged the "March on Washington for Jobs and Freedom," drawing between 200,000 and 300,000 marchers to the nation's capital and ending with

Martin Luther King Jr.'s historic "I Have a Dream" speech.

Kennedy had avoided military showdowns in Cuba and Berlin and received credit as a global peacemaker. He had helped to establish the Limited Nuclear Test Ban Treaty. If he could reach out to the Soviets and change the nature of their relationship, he could change the course of history.

Congress needed to ratify the nuclear test ban treaty, which wasn't a sure thing in 1963. Republican senator Barry Goldwater of Arizona argued that the test ban was weak on Soviet verification. After a month of hearings, the treaty was finally approved by the Senate Foreign Relations Committee and then the full Senate. On October 7, Kennedy added his signature, making the ban law.

The Cold War seemed to be warming. The CIA reported that the Soviets were on the verge of abandoning any plans they may have had to send a human to the moon. In truth, they were still trying to devise a moon rocket.

NASA director Webb strongly objected to the idea of collaborating with the Soviets on a moonshot. He said Project Apollo was on track and America needed no help from the Soviets whatsoever. He thought the Soviet plan was a trick, and agreeing to it would lead Congress to cut NASA's budget. Though the overall federal budget had been passed on August 11, Congress still had the ability to make adjustments and reduce NASA's funding.

Vice President Lyndon Johnson urged Kennedy to drop the idea of working with the Soviet Union and warned against mentioning the idea publicly. But Kennedy had already decided to raise the idea of a joint moonshot in an upcoming United Nations speech.

On September 20, Kennedy addressed the United Nations. He opened his remarks by heralding the Limited Nuclear Test Ban Treaty, which had by that time been signed by more than one hundred countries. When the president listed recent positive diplomatic developments between the United States and the Soviet Union, he was met with thunderous applause.

Halfway through his speech, he raised the issue of space. "In a field where the United States and the Soviet Union have a special capacity—in the field of space—there is room for new cooperation," the president said. "I include among these possibilities a joint expedition to the moon."

Kennedy reminded his audience that the United Nations had already declared that space belonged to all countries and international law would apply. "Why, therefore, should man's first flight to the moon be a matter of national competition?" he asked. "Why should the United States and the Soviet Union, in preparing for such expeditions, become involved in immense duplications of research, construction, and expenditure? Surely we should explore whether the scientists and astronauts of our two countries—indeed of all the world—cannot work together in the conquest of space, sending some day in this decade to the moon not the representatives of a single nation, but the representatives of all of our countries."

Nobody had seen Kennedy's proposal coming. United Nations delegates cheered, but in Washington, the news stunned lawmakers of both parties. White House advisors, the CIA, and other agencies were flabbergasted. This was a proposal to Khrushchev with world governments as a witness.

Khrushchev was silent in response.

Hearing no support from Moscow, Kennedy backed away from his bold proposal. Later, he said the Soviet Union didn't seem eager to enter the kind of relationship that would make the joint mission a success.

NASA officials were angry that Kennedy was using Project Apollo as a bargaining chip with the Soviets. A group of Republicans in Congress moved to ban the use of NASA funds for any cooperative effort toward a moon mission with the Soviet Union. As NASA officials had feared, Congress then renewed the battle over the agency's budget. Some wanted to cut space funding outright, to save money. Others wanted to move a billion dollars from NASA to the Air Force's space projects. In the end, the initial request of $5.7 billion was knocked down to $5.3 billion.

On October 25, Kennedy finally received an official answer from the Kremlin about his United Nations proposal. Khrushchev not only rejected the idea of cooperating on a moon mission but announced that his country wasn't interested in a moonshot at all.

This news gave NASA's critics even more reason to push for cutting funding. Why continue to pay for the moon race if no one else was running? Kennedy answered that Apollo had to continue on schedule to show that America wasn't influenced in the least by anything Moscow did. While the damage could have been worse, NASA's budget ended up being cut by another $300 million when Congress's supplementary budget bill was passed in December.

chapter twenty-five

Task Accomplished

On November 16, 1963, President John F. Kennedy went to Cape Canaveral to be briefed on Project Apollo and to see Wernher von Braun's two-stage Saturn C-1 vehicle. During his visit, the president beamed with pride. This Saturn was slated to launch before Christmas (a date that was eventually moved to January 29, 1964), marking the first-ever test of the upper stage.

After visiting Florida, Kennedy and Jackie planned to head to Texas for a two-day swing through San Antonio, Houston, Fort Worth, Dallas, and Austin. He planned to talk about the Apollo mission—a popular topic with both conservative and moderate Democrats—and avoid the topic of civil rights.

On November 21, the president spoke at a dedication ceremony for the new U.S. Air Force School of Aerospace Medicine

On November 18, 1963, President John F. Kennedy watches the launch of a Polaris missile from the USS "Observational Island" military vessel off the coast of Cape Canaveral.

at Brooks Air Force Base in San Antonio. He discussed how space research would benefit the medical field, leading to innovations that would improve healthcare in America. Heart defibrillators, kidney dialysis machines, CAT and MRI scans, and other breakthroughs in healthcare were, in part, developed in the space program.

Speaking about the "new frontier of outer space," Kennedy ended his San Antonio oration by linking space, medicine, and the moonshot with an anecdote by Irish author Frank O'Connor, who'd recently published his memoir, *An Only Child*. With great relish, the president recounted that O'Connor wrote about "how, as a boy, he and his friends would wander the countryside, and when they came to an orchard wall that seemed too high and too doubtful to try and too difficult to permit their voyage to continue, they took off their hats and tossed them over the wall—and then they had no choice but to follow them. This Nation has tossed its cap over the wall of space, and we have no choice but to follow it," Kennedy said. "Whatever the difficulties, they will be overcome."

That evening the Kennedys flew to Houston, where 10,000 people greeted them at the airport and thousands more lined the route downtown. President Kennedy spoke at the League of United Latin American Citizens banquet, followed by a gala dinner honoring Congressman Albert Thomas, whose advocacy had been crucial to winning congressional support of NASA's Manned Spacecraft Center. Jackie Kennedy had a wonderful time.

After the event, the Kennedys flew to Forth Worth. In his briefcase, Kennedy carried the draft of a speech he was planning to make the next afternoon to the Dallas Citizens Council at the Trade Mart convention center. His remarks focused on the New Frontier's belief in U.S. space supremacy. In part, he had planned to celebrate the fact that America had launched more than 130 vehicles into orbit around the Earth. "This effort is expensive—but it pays its own way, for freedom and for America, for there is no longer any fear in the free world that a Communist lead in space will become a permanent assertion of supremacy and the basis of military superiority," the president wrote. "There is no longer any doubt about the strength and skill of American science, American industry, American education, and the American free enterprise system. In short, our national space effort represents a great gain in, and a great resource of, our national strength."

On the morning of November 22, the Kennedys headed for Dallas. The president did not expect to receive the same kind of warm welcome he had in Houston and San Antonio, because Dallas hadn't benefited from as many NASA contracts. Kennedy was also quite unpopular with the area's conservatives.

At 11:55 a.m. Central Standard Time, the presidential motorcade left Love Field in Dallas for the ten-mile drive through downtown. Jack and Jackie rode in an open convertible, waving to the cheering crowds.

At 12:20 p.m., three shots rang out as the car passed Dealey

Plaza in downtown Dallas. Bullets entered President Kennedy's neck and head as he collapsed toward his wife.

At 1:00 p.m., President John Fitzgerald Kennedy was declared dead at Parkland Memorial Hospital. His lifeless body was carried out to Air Force One. Before the plane left for Washington, D.C., Lyndon Johnson took the oath of office of the U.S. presidency, administered by U.S. district judge Sarah Hughes.

In addition to his wife and two young children, Kennedy was survived by his father, Joseph, and mother, Rose. It's a terrible thing for parents to have to bury their own child.

Astronaut John Glenn was driving home from Ellington Field Joint Reserve Base near Houston when he heard the horrible news on his radio. He met up with his wife, Annie, and together they wept. "In the days that followed, as the initial shock and grief receded, Annie and I sat back as we had after Pearl Harbor and assessed our responsibilities to each other and to the country," Glenn said. "It was a time for soul searching."

That evening, Soviet Premier Nikita Khrushchev had just finished dinner when he was told that Kennedy had been shot. When he learned the details a few minutes later, the premier openly wept. The Soviet secret service told Khrushchev they believed right-wing extremists, angry at the possibility of improved relations with the Soviet Union, were responsible for the murder.

Astronaut Neil Armstrong was driving from Pensacola,

Florida, to Houston when he heard the news. Although Armstrong and Kennedy had never met, their legacies were forever bound together by the moonshot challenge. In the coming years, Armstrong would first go into space on Gemini VII in 1965. Four years later, he would join the Apollo 11 mission and become the first man on the moon.

NASA scientist Wernher von Braun was devastated by news of the assassination. He and his wife had been scheduled to dine with Kennedy at the White House three days later. Instead, that became the date of Kennedy's funeral. Von Braun marked it with an X on his calendar but kept working on his Saturn rocket.

Just days after her husband's death, Jacqueline Kennedy visited the new president, Lyndon Johnson, and the new first lady, Claudia "Lady Bird" Johnson, in the Oval Office. Jacqueline asked Johnson if he would honor her husband by renaming the site of NASA's space launches in Florida from Cape Canaveral to Cape Kennedy. She worried that without a reminder, Americans would forget about the moon pledge.

On November 28, President Johnson fulfilled Jacqueline Kennedy's wish at the end of his Thanksgiving message to the nation. Via Executive Order 11129, NASA's Civilian Launch Operation Center on the Florida coast would be renamed the John F. Kennedy Space Center. Taking things a step further, Johnson also ordered that the military-run Cape Canaveral station (station No. 1 of Atlantic Missile Range) also be part of the new Kennedy Space Center. To help differentiate the double honor, the Air Force renamed the military launch site Cape Kennedy Air Force Station. These were the first official actions taken by the U.S. government to permanently honor John F. Kennedy.

On January 29, 1964, the very Saturn rocket that Kennedy had inspected the week before his death was successfully tested at the Kennedy Space Center. Before takeoff, Wernher von Braun had engraved the initials "JFK" on a corner of the massive rocket. The spacecraft achieved an altitude of over 11,185 miles and a reentry speed of greater than 7 miles per second. If Kennedy had lived, this would have been the day he knew the moon was truly in reach by the end of the decade—and maybe even during his second White House term.

NASA was lucky to have a rocket engineer as talented as von Braun to work on Apollo. He and his Huntsville team not only designed the rockets that brought Americans to the moon but, later, also oversaw development of the space shuttle's propulsion system. But von Braun shouldn't be remembered as an American hero. His direct role in the Nazi concentration camp labor programs, where thousands perished under inhuman conditions, will—and should—forever taint his legacy. As historian Michael J. Neufeld summarized in *German Studies Review*, "von Braun made a Faustian bargain with the German Army and National Socialist [Nazi] regime in order to pursue his long-term dream of exploring space, and late in World War II found out what that bargain meant. His career, however admirable in many other aspects, serves as an exemplary warning of the dangers of the amoral pursuit of science and technology in the twentieth century—and the twenty-first."

After the January 29 Apollo launch, von Braun sent a letter of condolence to Jacqueline Kennedy. She returned a handwritten note on her personal stationery. It read:

February 11, 1964

Dear Dr. von Braun

I so thank you for your letter—about the Saturn—and about my husband. What a wonderful world it was for a few years—with men like you to help realize his dreams for this country—And you with a President who admired and understood you—so that together you changed the way the world looked at America—and made us proud again.

Please do me one favor—sometimes when you are making an announcement about some spectacular new success—say something about President Kennedy and how he helped turn the tide—so people won't forget.

I hope I am not the only one to feel this way—It is my only consolation—that at least he was given time to do some great work on this earth, which now seems such a miserable and lonely place without him.

How much more he could have done—but I must not think about that.

I do thank you for your letter.

Sincerely,
Jacqueline Kennedy

• • •

For the next four years, President Lyndon Johnson and NASA director James Webb defended Kennedy's Apollo moonshot pledge. In January 1967, the space program took a serious hit when an on-the-ground accident during an Apollo 1 launch rehearsal at Cape Canaveral killed astronauts Gus Grissom, Roger Chaffee, and Ed White. But the Apollo mission continued. On November 9, 1967, von Braun's Saturn V moon rocket made its first successful launch from Kennedy Space Center in Florida.

On July 20, 1969, the lunar module Eagle reached the moon, and Neil Armstrong and Buzz Aldrin became the first humans to set foot on the lunar surface. Armstrong famously said "that's one small step for [a] man, one giant leap for mankind." Two and a half hours later, just before climbing up the ladder of the Eagle to prep for leaving the moon, Armstrong asked Aldrin if he'd deposited the NASA-sanctioned memento they planned to leave behind. Aldrin, grateful for the reminder, reached into his shoulder pocket, pulled out a small package, and placed it on the moon. Inside the packet were a number of objects commemorating both American astronauts and Soviet cosmonauts: an Apollo 1 patch honoring Gus Grissom, Ed White, and Roger Chaffee, and shiny medals honoring Yuri Gagarin (the first human to orbit the Earth, who'd perished in a 1968 test-flight crash) and Vladimir Komarov (the first human to die in a space flight, after his Soyuz 1 reentry parachute failed to open in 1967). The packet also

The Apollo 11 rocket is on its mobile launch platform just after rollout from the Vehicle Assembly Building at the Kennedy Space Center, Cape Canaveral, Florida, on its way to Launch Complex 39A. The photograph was taken on May 17, 1969. Apollo 11, the first manned lunar landing mission, was launched on July 16, 1969, with astronauts Neil Armstrong, Edwin "Buzz" Aldrin, and Michael Collins on board.

contained a gold olive branch pin, symbolic of the peaceful nature of Apollo 11. To this day, the satchel still rests there in the lunar dust.

Four days later, the Apollo 11 command module Columbia brought the astronauts home safely. "This is the greatest week in the history of the world since the creation," President Richard Nixon told the astronauts. "As a result of what you've done, this world has never been closer together before."

NASA had triumphed. Wernher von Braun's life work in space had been realized. The lunar module that Kennedy had approved in 1962 had worked flawlessly. When word arrived that the Apollo 11 astronauts were all safe after splashdown in the Pacific, a quote from JFK's May 1961 address to Congress appeared on a large screen at Apollo mission control in Houston:

"I believe that this nation should commit itself to achieving the goal, before the decade is out, of landing a man on the moon and returning him safely to the earth."

On another screen, above the Apollo 11 logo, appeared the greatest tribute to John F. Kennedy's life and career:

"Task Accomplished, July 1969."

At around that time, an unknown citizen had left a lovely bouquet of flowers on Kennedy's Arlington National Cemetery grave with a card that read: "Mr. President, the Eagle has landed."

The three astronauts chosen for Apollo 11, the first manned lunar landing mission. From left to right: Edwin "Buzz" Aldrin, born in Montclair, New Jersey, in 1930; Michael Collins, born in Rome, Italy, in 1930; and Neil Armstrong, born in Wapakoneta, Ohio, in 1930. These space heroes made President John F. Kennedy's dream a reality.

Source Notes

Chapter 1: The New Ocean

"I believe that this nation . . ." Special Message by the President on Urgent National Needs: John F. Kennedy Speech to Congress, May 25, 1961.

"grandstanding play . . ." William E. Burrows, *This New Ocean: The Story of the First Space Age* (New York: Random House, 1998), p. 329.

"You don't run for president in your forties . . ." Ibid.

"New Ocean . . ." John F. Kennedy: Address at Rice University, September 12, 1962. John F. Kennedy Library. www.jfklibrary.org/JFK/Historic-Speeches/Multilingual-Rice-University-Speech.aspx

"Both the Soviet Union and the United States believed . . ."

Neil Armstrong, "Introduction," in Jay Barbree, Alan Shepard, and Deke Slayton, *Moon Shot: The Inside Story of America's Apollo Moon Landings* (Atlanta: Turner Publishing, 1994), p. 8–9.

"Kennedy's Apollo moonshot plan was more than just a reaction to Soviet successes in space . . ." John M. Logsdon, John F. Kennedy and the Race to the Moon (New York: Palgrave Macmillan, 2010) p. 8.

"the lack of effort, the lack of initiative . . ." John M. Logsdon, *John F. Kennedy and the Race to the Moon* (New York: Palgrave Macmillan, 2010), p. 8.

"We choose to go to the moon in this decade . . ." Papers of John F. Kennedy. Presidential Papers. President's Office Files. Speech Files. Address at Rice University, Houston, Texas, 12 September 1962.

"We set sail on this new sea . . ." Address at Rice University.

"The eyes of the world now look into space . . ." Public Papers of Presidents of the United States: John F. Kennedy, 1962.

Chapter 2: Reaching beyond the Sky

"supervise and direct the scientific study of the problems of flight . . ." James R. Hansen, *First Man: The Life of Neil A. Armstrong* (New York: Simon & Schuster, 2005), p. 130.

"lacked the knowledge ladled out . . ." "A Severe Strain on Credulity," *New York Times*, January 13, 1920.

"So much for the *New York Times* . . ." Quoted in "Frequently Asked Questions About Dr. Robert H. Goddard." Clark University Archives and Special Collections, www.clarku.edu/research/archives/goddard/faq.cfm.

"I bet you that the first man to walk on the moon . . ." Ernst Stuhlinger, "How It All Began—Memories of an Old-Timer," July 20, 1999. Wernher von Braun Library of Archives, U.S. Space & Rocket Center.

Chapter 3: Rocketing into Battle

"Peace in Our Time," John F. Kennedy (unsigned), "Peace in Our Time," the *Harvard Crimson*, October 9, 1939.

"astonishing theoretical knowledge . . ." Bob Ward, *Dr. Space: The Life of Wernher von Braun* (Annapolis, Maryland: Naval Institute Press, 2005), p. 18.

"If you want more money, you have to prove . . ." Walter R. Dornberger, "The German V-2," *Technology and Culture*, Vol. 4, No. 4, Autumn 1963, p. 397.

Chapter 4: Racing against the Third Reich

"a date which will live in infamy . . ." Franklin D. Roosevelt: 138—Address to Congress Requesting Declaration of War with Japan, December 8, 1941. The American Presidency Project, www.presidency.ucsb.edu/ documents/ address-congress-requesting-declaration-war-with-japan.

"buzz bombs," "Doodlebugs," Military History Now, "Buzz Kill—13 Remarkable Facts about the V-1 Flying Bomb," February 6, 2015. www.militaryhistorynow.com/2015/02/06/ buzz-kill-15-amazing-facts-about-the-v-1-flying-bomb/

"Survival," John Hersey, *New Yorker*, June 17, 1944; www.newyorker.com/magazine/1944/06/17/survival-2.

Chapter 5: Every Man for Himself

"This should never have happened . . ." Michael J. Neufeld, *Von Braun: Dreamer of Space, Engineer of War* (New York: Vintage, 2008), p. 184.

Chapter 6: A New Enemy

"The war made us get serious . . ." William Doyle, *PT 109: An American Epic of War, Survival, and the Destiny of John F. Kennedy* (New York: HarperCollins, 2015), p. xiii.

"What we do now will shape . . ." John F. Kennedy, congressional campaign radio broadcast, 1946, quoted in *John F. Kennedy in His Own Words*, edited by Eric Freedman and Edward Hoffman (New York: Citadel Press, 2005), p. 140.

"It seems to be a law of nature . . ." Christopher Potter, *The Earth Gazers: On Seeing Ourselves* (New York: Pegasus Books, 2018), p. 144; and Bob Ward, *Dr. Space: The Life of Wernher von Braun* (Annapolis, Maryland: Naval Institute Press, 2005) p. 13–15.

Chapter 7: And Then There Were Two

"Mr. Atomic Bomb . . ." James Mahaffey, *Atomic Awakening: A New Look at the History and Future of Nuclear Power* (New York: Pegasus Books, 2009), p. viii–x.

Chapter 8: Into the Space Race

"at a tempo for peace . . ." Bob Ward, *Dr. Space*, p. 74.

"the military-industrial complex . . ." Dwight Eisenhower, speech, April 16, 1953, "The Chance for Peace."

"There is little doubt but what the nation the first successfully landed . . ." Letter from Alan Dulles to Charles Erwin Wilson, January 29, 1955, CIA Library Reading Room, www.cia.gov/library/readingroom/docs/DOC_0006513734.pdf.

"missile gap . . ." Yanek Mieczkowski, *Eisenhower's Sputnik Moment: The Race for Space and World Prestige* (New York: Cornell University Press, 2013), p. 244.

"It is a contest to get a satellite into orbit . . ." "Space: Reach for the Stars," *Time*, Vol. 71, No. 7, February 17, 1958, p. 21–25.

Chapter 9: Sputnik Revolution

"I remember that he said the accident occurred . . ." Wernher von Braun, recorded interview by Walter D. Sohier and Eugene M. Emme, March 31, 1964, John F. Kennedy Oral History Program, p. 1.

"He had been following the work . . ." Ibid., p. 2.

"artificial moon . . ." William J. Jorden, "Soviets Fire Earth Satellite into Space: 560 Miles High," *New York Times*, October 5, 1957, p. 1.

"The Roman Empire controlled the world . . ." Lyndon Johnson, *The Vantage Point: Perspectives of the Presidency, 1963–69* (New York: Holt, 1971), p. 275–76.

"the age of Sputnik . . ." Papers of John F. Kennedy, Pre-Presidential Papers. Senate Files. Speeches and the Press. Speech Files, 1953–1960. Blue Key Banquet, University of Florida, Gainesville, Florida, 18 October 1957. JFKSEN-0898-018. John F. Kennedy Presidential Library and Museum.

"losing the satellite and missile race . . ." Christopher A. Preble, "Who Ever Believed in the Missile Gap?" John F. Kennedy and the Politics of National Security, *Presidential Studies Quarterly*, 33(4), p. 801–826.

"Muttnik," "Poochnik," Bob Kealing, *Kerouac in Florida: Where the Road Ends* (Arbiter Press, 2004), p. 30.

"outstripped the leading capitalist country . . ." William Taubman, *Khrushchev: The Man and His Era* (New York: W.W. Norton, 2003), p. 378.

"a battle more important and great . . ." Robert A. Divine,
*The Sputnik Challenge: Eisenhower's Response to the Soviet
Satellite* (New York: Oxford University Press, 1993),
p. xv–vvi.

"It is now apparent that we could have been first . . ."
Papers of John F. Kennedy, Pre-Presidential Papers.
Senate Files. Speeches and the Press. Speech Files, 1953–
1960. Kansas Democratic Club Banquet. Topeka, Kansas,
6 November 1957. JFKSEN-0898-027. John F. Kennedy
Presidential Library and Museum.

"It's the Americans' turn now . . ." "U.S. Turn Now,
Bulganin Says," *New York Times*, November 12, 1957, p. 27.

"did not come as a surprise . . ." James Hagerty response to
Sputnik. John Foster Dulles to James C. Hagerty, October
8, 1957: "Draft Statements on the Soviet Satellite," October
5, 1957. John Foster Dulles Papers, Dwight D. Eisenhower
Library, Abilene, Kansas. www.history.nasa.gov/
sputnik/15.html. See also *Dwight D. Eisenhower: The
White House Years, vol. 2: Waging Peace: 1956–1961* (New
York: Doubleday, 1965)

"For God's sake turn us loose . . ." Michael J. Neufield, Von
Braun (New York: Vintage Books, 2008), p. 312.

Chapter 10: Keeping Up with the Kremlin

"small satellite spheres . . ." Constance McLaughlin Green and Milton Lomask, *Project Vanguard: The NASA History* (Mineola, New York: Dover Publications, 2009), p. 198.

"Kaputnik," "Stayputnik," "Flopnik," Paul Dixon, *Sputnik: The Shock of the Century* (New York: Walker Books Publishing Co., 2001), p. 250.

"the flaunting of the Soviets of their ability . . ." Papers of John F. Kennedy, Pre-Presidential Papers. Senate Files. Speeches and the Press. Speech Files, 1953–1960. Woman's Club of Richmond, Virginia, 20 January 1958. JFKSEN-0899-005. John F. Kennedy Presidential Library and Museum.

"was immersed in . . ." James R. Hansen, *First Man: The Life of Neil A. Armstrong* (New York: Simon & Schuster, 2005), p. 53.

Chapter 11: Closing the Gap

"It makes us feel that we paid . . ." John B. Medaris, *Countdown for Decision* (New York: G. P. Putnam, 1960), pp. 143–73.

"I sure feel a lot better now . . ." Yanek Mieczkowski, *Eisenhower's Sputnik Moment: The Race for Space and World Prestige* (New York: Cornell University Press, 2013), p. 129.

"grapefruit satellite . . ." Green and Lomask, *Project Vanguard*, p. 187.

"Americans were no longer the paramount power . . ." Papers of John F. Kennedy. Pre-Presidential Papers. Senate Files. Speeches and the Press. Speech Files, 1953–1960. Eighth Annual Pittsburgh World Affairs Forum, Pittsburgh, Pennsylvania, 18 April 1958. JFKSEN-0900-021. John F. Kennedy Presidential Library and Museum.

"Our nation could have afforded . . ." Preble, *Presidential Studies Quarterly*, p. 801–826.

"information as to discoveries . . ." John M. Logsdon (ed.), *Exploring the Unknown: Selected Documents in the History of the U.S. Civil Space Program*. Vol. 1 (Washington, D.C.: NAA, 1996), p. 334–45.

"The balance sheet of a year of effort . . ." Hanson W. Baldwin, "The Sputnik Era—Where the U.S. and Soviet Union Stand," *New York Times*, October 5, 1958, p. E6.

Chapter 12: Mercury Seven to the Rescue

"It is my pleasure to introduce to you . . ." John Logsdon and Roger D. Luanis, *Exploring the Unknown: Selected Documents in the History of the U.S. Civil Space Program*, Vol VII (National Aeronautics and Space Administration NASA History Division, Washington, D.C., 2008), p. 17–18. www.history.nasa.gov/SP-4407vol7Chap1.pdf.

"Magnificent Seven," Michael Collins, *Carrying the Fire: An Astronaut's Journeys* (New York: Farrar, Straus, and Giroux, 1974), p. 27.

"They spoke of 'duty' and 'faith' and 'country' . . ." Reston in Roger D. Launius, *The Smithsonian History of Space Exploration: From the Ancient World to the Extraterrestrial Future* (Washington, D.C.: Smithsonian Books, 2018), p. 107.

"Man is still the best computer . . ." Charles R. Pellegrino and Joshua Stoff, *Chariots for Apollo: The Untold Story Behind the Race to the Moon* (New York: Avon Books, 1999), p. 15.

Chapter 13: Kennedy for President

"a serious man on a serious mission . . ." Thurston Clarke, *JFK's Last Hundred Days: The Transformation of a Man and the Emergence of a Great President* (Westminster, UK: Penguin Publishing Group, 2014), p. 343.

"Jack was always out kissing babies . . ." John T. Shaw, *JFK in the Senate: Pathway to the Presidency* (Maryland: Stackpole Books, 1976), p. 183.

"Saturn was the next outer planet in the solar system . . ." Erik Bergaust, *Wernher von Braun* (Stackpole Books, 2015), p. 406.

"I thought the image of the god Apollo . . ." Courtney G. Brooks, James M. Grimwood, and Lloyd S. Swenson Jr., *Chariot for Apollo: The NASA History of Manned Lunar Spacecraft to 1969*, The NASA History Series, NASA Sp-4205 (Washington, D.C.: National Aeronautics and Space Administration Scientific and Technical Information Office, 1979), p. 15.

"little scrawny fellow with rickets . . ." Larry Tye, *Bobby Kennedy: The Making of a Liberal Icon* (New York: Random House, 2016), p. 111.

"an uneasy and joyless marriage of convenience . . ." Richard Nixon, *RN: The Memoirs of Richard Nixon* (NY: Grosset and Dunlap, 1978), p. 215.

"The New Frontier of which I speak . . ." John F. Kennedy: "Address of Senator John F. Kennedy Accepting the Democratic Party Nomination for the Presidency of the United States—Memorial Coliseum, Los Angeles," July 15, 1960. Online by Gerhard Peters and John T. Woolley, The American Presidency Project. www.presidency.ucsb.edu/documents/address-senator-john-f-kennedy-accepting -the-democratic-party-nomination-for-the

"The people of the world respect . . ." John F. Kennedy speech at Portland, Oregon, September 7, 1960. American Presidency Project, Speech of Senator John F. Kennedy at Multnomah Hotel, September 7, 1960. www.presidency. ucsb.edu/ws/index.php?pid=25675

"with too many slums, with too few schools . . ." American Presidency Project: Address of Senator John F. Kennedy to the Greater Houston Ministerial Association, September 12, 1960. www.jfklibrary.org/Asset-Viewer/ ALL6YEBJMEKYGMCntnSCvg.aspx

"I am tired of reading . . ." John F. Kennedy, "Speech by Senator John F. Kennedy at a Democratic Fund-Raising Dinner in Syracuse, N.Y.," September 29, 1960, Kennedy Library, www.jfklibrary.org/asset-viewer/archives/ JFKSEN/0912/JFKSEN-0912-021.

Chapter 14: Setting the Course at NASA

"Let the word go forth . . ." John F. Kennedy, "Inaugural Address," January 20, 1961. Online by Gerhard Peters and John T. Woolley, The American Presidency Project. www.presidency.ucsb.edu/ws?pid=8032.

"Ask not what your country can do . . ." Ibid.

Chapter 15: The First Men in Space

"It is a fact that it is going to take some time . . ." John F. Kennedy: "The President's News Conference," April 12, 1961. Online by Gerhard Peters and John T. Woolley, The American Presidency Project. www.presidency.ucsb.educ/ws?pid=8055

"the most expensive funeral man has ever had . . ." Quoted in Francis French and Colin Burgess, *Into That Silent Sea: Trailblazers of the Space Era, 1961–1965* (Lincoln: University of Nebraska Press, 2009), p. 57.

"dramatic accomplishments in space are being . . ." John F. Kennedy Library: Memorandum from Vice President Johnson to President Kennedy on the Space Program April 28, 1961. www.jfklibrary.org/Asset-Viewer/DjiWpQJegkuIlX7WZAUCtQ.aspx.

"We cannot expect the Russians to transfer . . ." Vice
President Lyndon B. Johnson memorandum to President
John F. Kennedy, April 28, 1961. John F. Kennedy Library:
Memorandum from Vice President Johnson to President
Kennedy on the Space Program April 28, 1961. www.
jfklibrary.org/AssetViewer/DjiWpQJegkuIlX7WZAUCtQ.
aspx.

"Why don't you fix your little problem . . ." Noble Wilford,
"Alan B. Shepard, Jr. Is Dead at 74. First American Space
Traveler," *New York Times*, July 23, 1998.

"the greatest 'suspense drama' in the history of TV,"
Howard Stentz, "Space Shot Top Television Thriller,"
Houston Chronicle, May 5, 1961, p. 16.

"substantially larger effort . . ." News Conference 11, May
5, 1961. Kennedy Library, www.jfklibrary.org/archives/
other-resources/john-f-kennedy-press-conferences/
news-conference-11.

Chapter 16: We're Going to the Moon

"Urgent National Needs . . ." Roger D. Launius (ed.), *The
U.S. Space Program and American Society* (MA: Discovery
Enterprises, 1998), p. 22.

"The Space Plan," James D. Outzen, *The Dorian Files Revealed: A Compendium of the NRO's Manned Orbiting Laboratory Documents*. www.nro.gov/Portals/65/ documents/history/csnr/programs/docs/MOL_ Compendium_August_2015.pdf

"end of the decade . . ." Mike Wall, "The Moon and the Man at 50: Why JFK's Space Exploration Speech Still Resonates." SPACE.com, May 25, 2011.

"For while we cannot guarantee . . ." Special Message by the President on Urgent National Needs: John F. Kennedy Speech to Congress, May 25, 1961. www.catalog.archives. gov/id/193915.

"I believe this nation should commit . . ." Ibid.

"our debt may reach the moon before we do," Public Debt Limit Hearing Before the Committee on Finance. United States Senate, Eighty-Seventh Congress (Washington, D.C.: U.S. Government Printing Office, 1961).

"I taught Jack better . . ." Joseph P. Kennedy Sr. quoted in Michael R. Beschloss, *The Crisis Years: Kennedy and Khrushchev, 1960–1963* (New York: HarperCollins, 1991), p. 166.

Chapter 17: Gearing Up for a Lunar Voyage

"The gap between a twenty-minute up-and-down . . ." Alok Jha, "Neil Armstrong Breaks His Silence to Give Accountants Moon Exclusive," *Guardian*, May 23, 2012.

"The costs will be tremendous . . ." Senator Robert S. Kerr remarks at the Conference on the Peaceful Use of Space Meeting in Tulsa, 26 May, 1961, John F. Kennedy Presidential Library and Museum.

"Landlords will not rent to them . . ." Edward R. Murrow, May 24, 1961, National Press Club Luncheon Speakers, Library of Congress Recorded Sound Research Center.

"If we cooperate, it will mean . . ." James Schefter, *The Race: The Complete True Story of How America Beat Russia to the Moon* (New York: Doubleday, 1999), p. 145.

Chapter 18: Laying the Groundwork

"It won't happen again," United Press International, "U.S. Orbit Shot Next Year to Avoid Tape 'Booboo,'" *Cumberland* (Maryland) *Evening Times*, July 26, 1961.

Chapter 19: Godspeed, John Glenn

"It's not a very nice solution . . ." John Lewis Gaddis, *The Cold War: A New History* (London, Penguin Press, 2005), p. 115.

"less than a 50-50 chance," John Troan, "January Still Target of Moon Shot; 2 Test Failures May Not Delay On-Spot Probe," *Pittsburgh Press*, November 21, 1961, p. 24.

"This nation belongs among the first . . ." "Transcript of the President's Address to Congress on Domestic and World Affairs," *New York Times*, January 12, 1962, p. 12.

"Godspeed John Glenn," Barbara Maranzani, "7 Things You May Not Know About John Glenn," History.com, www.history.com/news/7-things-you-may -notknow-about-john-glenn-and-friendship-7.

"The distance to the moon . . ." Alan Shepard, Deke Slayton and Jay Barbree, *Moon Shot: The Inside Story of America's Race to the Moon* (Atlanta: Turner Publishing, 1994), p. 152.

"Around the World with Friendship 7," Teusel Muir-Harmony, "Friendship 7's 'Fourth Orbit'" in Michael J. Neufeld (ed.), *Milestones of Space: Eleven Iconic Objects*

from the Smithsonian National Air and Space Museum
(Minneapolis, MN, Zenith Press, 2014), p. 16–17.

Chapter 20: Peace in Space

"could render no greater service to mankind . . ." Papers of
John F. Kennedy. Presidential Papers. White House Staff
Files of Pierre Salinger. Subject Files, 1961–1964.
Khrushchev/Kennedy letters, 7 March 1962–2 January
1963. JFKWHSFPS-010-010. John F. Kennedy
Presidential Library and Museum.

"How can we guarantee that space will be used . . ." "Barry
Calls for All-Out Military Space Program," *Tucson Daily
Citizen*, July 17, 1962, p. 6.

"gambling with national survival . . ." John G. Norris,
"Senate Hears Demands for Building Strong Military
Capability," *Washington Post*, August 21, 1962, p. A1.

"This is the vehicle designed to fulfill . . ." "JFK Sees
Saturn Test at Huntsville Center," *Montgomery Advertiser*,
September 12, 1962, p. 1.

"We shall be first!" Bob Ward, *Dr. Space*, p. 132.

Chapter 21: Not Because It Is Easy

"I do not know whether the people of the Southwest . . ." *Houston Press*, September 12, 1962. NASA 1060s Vertical Files, Houston Metropolitan Research Center, Houston, Texas.

"Surely the opening vistas of space promise high costs . . ." JFK September 12 speech at Rice University. John F. Kennedy: Address at Rice University, September 12, 1962. John F. Kennedy Library, www.jfklibrary.org/JFK/Historic-Speeches/Multilingual-Rice-University-Speech.aspx.

"The exploration of space will go ahead . . ." Ibid.

"We choose to go to the moon . . ." John F. Kennedy: "Address at Rice University in Houston on the Nation's Space Effort," September 12, 1962. Online by Gerhard Peters and John T. Woolley, The American Presidency Project. www.presidency.ucsb.edu/ws/?pid=8862.

"All right, now you guys do the details!" Rory Kennedy (niece of JFK) and Sandy Kenyon (ABC News), October 16, 2017. Ted Sorensen told this story on Kenyon's "Focus on Youth" syndicated radio show.

"By all means, we must carry on our explorations of

space . . ." Dwight D. Eisenhower, "Are We Headed in the Wrong Direction," *Saturday Evening Post*, August 11, 1962, p. 24.

"Why the great hurry?" Alvin Spirak, "Pledge to Beat Russia to the Moon," *St. Louis Post-Dispatch*, September 13, 1962, p.1.

"Let me make this clear . . ." Papers of John F. Kennedy. Presidential Papers. President's Office Files. Press Conference. 13 September 1962. JFKOF-057-012/ John F. Kennedy Presidential Library and Museum.

Chapter 22: Winning at Any Cost

"Yes, sir . . ." James R. Hansen, *First Man: The Life of Neil A. Armstrong* (New York: Simon & Schuster, 2005), p. 202.

"Many women are employed in the program . . ." O.B. Lloyd Jr. to Susan Marie Scott, June 18, 1962, University of Houston—Clear Lake, NASA Archive Collection, No. 2018-0001.

"Mercury 13," Dianna Wray, "The Real Story of NASA's First Female Astronauts" *Miami New Times*, September 19, 2017.

"Not a fancy name like Freedom . . ." Francis French and Colin Burgess, *Into That Silent Sea: Trailblazers of the Space Era*, 1962–1965, p. 232.

"I think it is one of the top-priority programs . . ." "Transcript of Presidential Meeting in the Cabinet Room of the White House: Supplemental Appropriations for the National Aeronautics and Space Administration (NASA), November 21, 1962," John F. Kennedy Library President's Office Files, Presidential Recordings Collections, tape #63.

"I think it is the top priority . . ." Ibid.

"Everything that we do ought to really be tied . . ." Ibid.

"I have some feeling that you might not have been . . ." Ibid.

Chapter 23: Staying Moonbound

"anybody who would spend $40 billion . . ." Former President Eisenhower remark from his farm in Gettysburg—June 13, 1963.

"our space program has an overriding urgency . . ." John F. Kennedy to Lyndon Johnson, April 9, 1963, and Lyndon Johnson to John F. Kennedy, NASA Historical Reference Collection, Houston, Texas.

"future of society is at stake . . ." Ibid.

"One of the things which warmed us the most . . ."
"Remarks Upon Presenting the NASA Distinguished
Service Medal to Astronaut L. Gordon Cooper," May 21,
1963. Online by Gerhard Peters and John T. Woolley, The
American Presidency Project. www.presidency.ucsb.edu/
ws/?pid=9225.

"The United States, as the world knows . . ." Commencement
Address at American University in Washington: June 10,
1963, The American Presidency Project: John F. Kennedy.
www.presidency.ucsb.edu/ws/?pid=9266.

"the best speech by any president since Roosevelt . . ."
William Taubman, *Khrushchev: The Man and His Era*
(New York: W.W. Norton, 2003), p. 602.

"the right to be free . . ." President Kennedy Speech in West
Berlin "Ich bin ein Berliner" June 26, 1963.

"Freedom is indivisible . . ." Ibid.

Chapter 24: Astronauts and Cosmonauts Together

"a spectacular dash . . ." Dwight D. Eisenhower to Charles
Halleck, May 26, 1963, White House Presidents, NASA
History Office, Washington, D.C.

"The point of the matter always has been . . ." "News Conference 58" John F. Kennedy Library and Museum, www.jfklibrary.org/Historical+Resources/Archives.

"In a field where the United States and the Soviet Union . . ." John F. Kennedy: "Address Before the 18th General Assembly of the United Nations," September 20,1963. Online by Gerhard Peters and John T. Woolley, The American Presidency Project. www.presidency.ucsb. edu/ws/?pid=9416.

"Why, therefore, should man's first flight . . ." Ibid.

Chapter 25: Task Accomplished

"how, as a boy . . ." "Remarks at Aero-Space Medical Health Center Dedication, San Antonio, Texas, 21 November 1963," Papers of John F. Kennedy, Presidential Papers, President's Office Files, Speech Files, Kennedy Library.

"This effort is expensive . . ." Papers of John F. Kennedy. Presidential Papers. President's Office Files. Speech Files. Undelivered remarks for Dallas Citizens Council, Trade Mart, Dallas, Texas, 22 November 1963.

"In the days that followed . . ." John Glenn and Nick Taylor. *John Glenn: A Memoir* (New York: Bantam Books, 1999), p. 395.

"Von Braun made a Faustian bargain . . ." Michael J. Neufeld, "Wernher von Braun, the SS, and 'Concentration Camp Labor': Questions of Moral, Political, and Criminal Responsibility," *German Studies Review* 25/1 (February 2002). The quote is from a published letter he wrote defending his interpretation on December 2002, which appeared in "Wernher von Braun and Concentration Camp Labor: An Exchange" *German Studies Review* 26/1 (2003).

"Dear Dr. von Braun . . ." Wernher von Braun to Jacqueline Kennedy. Feb. 1, 1964, and Jacqueline Kennedy to Wernher von Braun, February 11, 1964. Wernher on Braun Library and Archives, U.S. Space & Rocket Center, Huntsville, Alabama.

"This is the greatest week in the history of the world since the creation," John M. Logsdon "Ten Presidents and NASA." https://www.nasa.gov/50th/50th_magazine/10presidents.html.

"I believe that this nation . . ." Special Message by the President on Urgent National Needs: John F. Kennedy Speech to Congress, May 25, 1961.

"Task Accomplished, July 1969," John M. Logsdon, *John F. Kennedy and the Race to the Moon* (New York: Palgrave Macmillan, 2010), p. 222.

"would be renamed Cape Kennedy . . ." Cabell Phillips, "Canaveral Space Center Renamed Cape Kennedy," *New York Times*, November 29, 1963, p. 1.

Bibliography

The "dean" of U.S. space history is John M. Logsdon. His books are invaluable to anybody interested in the American moonshot. Of special interest are his classic books *John F. Kennedy and the Race to the Moon* (New York: Palgrave Macmillan, 2010) and *After Apollo? Richard Nixon and the American Space Program* (New York: Palgrave Macmillan, 2015). Logsdon also served as editor for the seven-volume series *Exploring the Unknown*, which collects key documents from the history of the U.S. space program. Digital copies can be downloaded at www.history.nasa.gov/series95.html. NASA also offers a lengthy list of other publications at www.history.nasa.gov/publications.html.

The most knowledgeable scholar on NASA and the Cold War is Roger D. Launius. All of his space books are indispensable.

Both space history and Kennedy studies are very rich fields. Here is a boiled-down list of the books I found most helpful in my writing and research:

William E. Burrows, *This New Ocean: The Story of the First Space Age* (New York: Random House, 1998)

Andrew Chaikin, *A Man on the Moon: The Voyages of the Apollo Astronauts* (Penguin Books, 2007)

James R. Hansen, *First Man: The Life of Neil A. Armstrong* (Simon & Schuster, 2005)

Dennis Jenkins, *The Space Shuttle: Developing an Icon: 1972–2013* (Specialty Press, 2017)

Christopher Kraft, *Flight: My Life in Mission Control* (Dutton, 2001)

Gene Kranz, *Failure Is Not an Option: Mission Control from Mercury to Apollo 13 and Beyond* (Simon & Schuster, 2009)

W. Henry Lambright, *Powering Apollo: James E. Webb of NASA* (Johns Hopkins University Press, 1998)

Roger D. Launius and Howard E. McCurdy, *Spaceflight and the Myth of Presidential Leadership* (University of Illinois Press, 1997)

Roger D. Launius, *The Smithsonian History of Space Exploration* (Smithsonian Books, 2018)

Howard E. McCurdy, *Space and the American Imagination* (Johns Hopkins University Press, 2011)

————, *The Space Station Decision: Incremental Politics and Technological Choice* (Johns Hopkins University Press, 2007)

Walter A. McDougall, . . . *The Heavens and the Earth: A Political History of the Space Age* (Johns Hopkins University Press, 1997)

Yanek Mieczkowski, *Eisenhower's Sputnik Moment: The Race for Space and World Prestige* (Cornell University Press, 2013)

Charles Murray and Catherine Bly Cox, *Apollo: The Race To the Moon* (Simon & Schuster, 1989)

Michael J. Neufeld, *Von Braun: Dreamer of Space, Engineer of War* (Vintage, 2008)

Lynn Sherr, *Sally Ride: America's First Woman in Space* (Simon & Schuster, 2015)

Margot Lee Shetterly, *Hidden Figures: The American Dream and the Untold Story of the Black Woman Mathematicians Who Helped Win the Space Race* (William Morrow, 2016)

Neil deGrasse Tyson and Avis Lang, *Accessory to War: The Unspoken Alliance Between Astrophysics and the Military* (W.W. Norton, 2018)

Bob Ward, *Dr. Space: The Life of Wernher von Braun* (Naval Institute Press, 2005)

Margaret A. Weitekamp, *Right Stuff, Wrong Sex: America's First Women in Space Program* (Johns Hopkins University Press, 2005)

Tom Wolfe, *The Right Stuff* (Picador, 2008)

PHOTO CREDITS

Discover More
Young Readers' Editions

HARPER
An Imprint of HarperCollinsPublishers

www.harpercollinschildrens.com

Amistad
An Imprint of HarperCollinsPublishers